CLASSROOM
at THE END *of*
THE 'LINE'

Assembly Line Workers at
Midwest Community
and
Technical Colleges

SHARON A. KENNEDY

ISBN: 1484191080
ISBN 13: 9781484191088
Library of Congress Control Number: 2013908306
CreateSpace Independent Publishing Platform
North Charleston, South Carolina

Dedication

This book is dedicated to all the men and women who left the plants and, at a time of great upheaval in their lives, overcame their fear, stress, and anxiety to make it into the classroom and stay to completion. Educators applaud you and America appreciates you.

Elaine,
Thanks for coming!
Enjoy these Midwar
Stories!

Preface

When I tell people I am writing about Midwest assembly line workers going to college, I get a variety of responses. Most people say, "That sounds interesting." Some mean it. One said, "You really have a project on your hands!" I can tell that most cannot fathom why I would want to do this. Why does it matter?

In response, there are two answers. The more "official" answer is that this subject and its implications are important to the future of the country. Every major media outlet in the United States has reported on work of the community and technical colleges. Most US presidents over the past twenty years—including President Barack Obama as well as candidates for president and vice president—speak of upgrading the skills of the unskilled so they can fill positions, particularly in manufacturing. This is a bipartisan issue. This issue is of national concern.

But, on a more fundamental level, I write to memorialize the experience of the workers themselves and the college staff and faculty who served them. The workers who became students in quick order (employed one day, unemployed the next) give insights into the problems and challenges they face, which will continue to be encountered by others like them who follow. I conducted a total of forty-three interviews between 2010 and 2012. This book includes many excerpts from these interviews.

For the small colleges that experienced sharp enrollment increases and struggled to accommodate the masses immediately when plants closed, very practical lessons can be learned. For the larger community colleges that chose to get the workers in and out quickly through very specific non-credit shorter-term training, a different story of success and failure emerges. Michigan community colleges, for example, were trying to do the best they could within their structure and without adult basic education support. These are honest stories about what happened, the good and not-so-good.

Three colleges in the Midwest states of Wisconsin, Michigan, and Indiana were chosen as research sites. These colleges represent different models of two-year colleges. Blackhawk Technical College, where I am employed, is one of sixteen technical colleges in Wisconsin. The primary mission of the technical college is to prepare students for the workforce.

Montcalm Community College is one of twenty-eight community colleges in Michigan. Community colleges have a broader mission and often have more students transferring to a university than preparing for immediate employment.

Indiana has a unique system in the Midwest in that it has a greater emphasis on industry-recognized credentials as opposed to academic credit. Ivy Tech-Indianapolis is one of many campuses in the state with a significant short-term training emphasis for the many manufacturing companies in this district.

While it is dangerous to generalize about a very large group of students, the simple truth is that assembly line workers, who began losing their jobs in Michigan during the decade of the 2000s and in other states during the Great Recession, are different from most other students. The vast majority of these students suffered in ways that other students do not *because* they were former assembly-line workers. This is the essence of this collection of stories: how the students' former status influenced their work at the college and how the college was impacted by this same former status.[1]

---

[1] Names have been changed in the stories at Blackhawk Technical College in order to protect the privacy of those in the community and at the college.

Table of Contents

Introduction: Culture of the Assembly Line and Its Workers

Once the assembly line starts, the brain turns off.

Studs Terkel, *Working*

History

Henry Ford's concept of the assembly line is over one hundred years old. It single-handedly revolutionized industrial production and made it more efficient. In Ford's day, and well into present day, it brought the cost of an automobile down and allowed workers to be able to afford to purchase their own. That's typically viewed a good thing. But there is much disagreement on the impact of assembly line labor on workers over time.

Prior to the use of assembly lines, several workers produced one automobile and one-third of those workers were craftsmen. With the assembly line, however, people were no longer performing their craft. Personal freedoms of the worker, like freedom of movement and the ability to communicate with coworkers, were greatly diminished. Communication on the line among workers was generally discouraged and work was done in isolation. In Studs Terkel's book *Working*, a spot welder described his station: "You can work next to a guy for months without even knowing his name." He says you are too busy to talk and you can't hear. If you were to try to talk, you would have to holler in your coworker's ear.

In *Shop Class As Soulcraft*, Matthew Crawford states that craftsmen in the factory walked off the job when the assembly line was first introduced. In fact, Ford had to actually pay a higher daily rate, five dollars at the time, in order to keep workers on the job. The "line" separated thinking from doing, and craftsmen were demeaned.

Research on the origins of the assembly line credit a theory called "scientific management," where planning and design are done off of the plant floor, and assembly line workers need little knowledge or ability to execute production. Regardless of the motivation for this silo process, the separation of the assembly of distinct parts required that each worker perform one function for up to ten hours a day.

Ben Hamper, former assembly line worker at the Flint, Michigan, Truck and Coach Plant, states in *Rivethead: Tales for the Assembly Line* that working the line for General Motors in the early 1990s was something parents did so that their offspring wouldn't have to. Even though this thinking would change over the decades, one thing that was impossible to escape was the monotony of the jobs. "Every minute, every hour, every truck and every movement was a plodding replica of the one that had gone before," says Hamper, describing his own experience on what this does to brain cells.

Over the years, parents actually did encourage their offspring to go to work at the plant, and many did. The plants became safer and better places to work. Companies began to conduct research evaluating the "human factor," which brought about change to the ergonomics of workers and workplace design. One particular study reviewed the impact on the body of standing in one spot versus moving around in the work space. Other studies looked at changing job duties over a shift so that workers were not subjected to repetitive motion injuries. Plants went to a model of rotating jobs, which required that different muscles be used. The company realized it was in everyone's best interest to prevent workers from incurring injuries.

Henry Ford could not have known that changes in technology over the next nine decades would mean that robots would replace workers where rote work allowed, and the remaining work would be done by those who would use a computer to program those robots, needing an understanding in physics and math to do so. The *doing*, therefore, now requires *a lot* of thinking. Furthermore, as the model moved to people working in teams and communicating often to solve problems, companies now require those skills that eighty years of assembly work essentially erased in workers. Those workers who adapted to the changes would be required to go college to acquire additional skills.

Impact of Work on Workers
Who Became Students

Very little research has been done on how assembly line work impacts the brain and learning. Where previous craftspeople had to make a product using a skill that required a thought process, assembly lines require little skill while performing the same repetitive function, and little thought is engendered. Hamper, in *Rivethead,* describes entire shifts sailing by during which he "hardly developed a tangible current of thought."

Assembly line workers who came to college described how they dealt with the boredom and mind-numbing nature of the work. They also worried that their brains had turned to "mush." While there were workers, like Hamper, who embraced the fact that they did not have to think while they worked, others hated the job because of this. Some, where allowed, used headphones, listened to music, or reminisced to pass the day.

For workers who later became students, all of this passive activity was about to change. For example, fortunately or unfortunately, the expected level of communication between teacher and student, and student to student, was high in the educational setting. This was one of many skills they would need to learn.

Part I – The Technical College: Workforce Technical Education

The Place:	Janesville, Wisconsin
The Plant:	General Motors
The Sites:	The Rock County Job Center
	Blackhawk Technical College

The General Motors Plant in the Cornfields

An 'Unofficial' History

The Janesville General Motors plant started as a farm implement tractor factory in 1899. In 1918, General Motors purchased the manufacturing plant. In 1923, production of Chevrolets began. During World War II, it stopped making automobiles and made bullet shells. The lines changed over time. Some were added, such as the sport-utility vehicle line. Some lines went away. By 2008, sport-utility vehicle sales were sagging and while the buildings were renovated many times, they never received the production modernization others had.

According to retirees from the plant who were interviewed (together they had over one hundred years of employment), the plant was known nationally as having a quality workforce. It employed farmers who farmed during the day and worked second shift at the plant. It employed people who had bachelor's and master's degrees and stayed because of the good paycheck (sometimes called "golden handcuffs"). It employed people who came to the plant directly out of high school and expected to retire from there. (Anecdotally there is also a persistent rumor about a worker who actually lived at the plant for a period of time after his divorce. This rumor could not be confirmed.)

Some assemblyline workers were illiterate, and some better at hiding it than others. One such worker was a farmer, who had his wife do all of his paper work. He was fine until the company wanted to make him a supervisor, and he could no longer hide.

Under a UAW national agreement in the 1990s, a basic skills center came into existence at the Janesville plant. The company was aware that basic literacy skills were needed. In the past, someone could show a worker how to do something; now workers had to read the instructions. Workers needed reading skills. There was also the ever-changing world of technology at the plant; much of the work had become computer-based. Some of the 'build sheets' required specific parts and equipment calibration.

In addition to the basic skills center, the Janesville plant also became the plant in the 1990s that utilized the most tuition assistance of all GM's plants. Many actually believed it had the most educated GM workforce. Ten percent of the workers who came to Blackhawk Technical College after the closure had been there before. They had been taking one course at a time, whenever a ten-hour workday didn't cut into their ability to take classes.

One thing is clear, though: Assembly line work, generally, was in no way conducive to promotion of collaboration and communication skills. Those workers who applied for and were selected to work with the local or international UAW union, who received consistent continuing education training, who were on the contract negotiating team, and who generally took on greater leadership roles were the exceptions. These workers did not remain on the line. They found ways to get off the line and their workdays were more varied and interesting. Furthermore, they were encouraged, and in some cases mandated, to participate in professional development. Thus, their learning did not stop at the front door of the plant on their first day. Over the years, they forced themselves to learn new things.

In the early 1990s, when GM built the larger vehicles, the Janesville plant made the company a significant amount of money on each car, according to some employees. It was, after all, the bigger models that produced the most profits. This profit enabled GM to expand and produce in the global marketplace. Some Janesville workers saw the irony of this situation. They believed the same global expansion eventually led to their jobs being eliminated.

Over the years, the workforce declined. The plant once employed about 7,300 people. In 1985, it was announced that the Janesville plant was no longer going to build pick-up trucks, instead transferring production to a new plant in Indiana. Twelve hundred people from Janesville moved to Fort Wayne. By the time the Janesville plant closed, it had already begun cutting back on tuition assistance and it employed only one shift of 1,250 people. According to the *Janesville Gazette*, on December 23, 2008, the last SUV rolled off the line.

The anger of the employees at the corporation at the time of closure was palpable. People who were not ready to retire had no choice. Employees who were not accustomed to making significant financial decisions or planning for their future took the buy-out and ended up spending it. For others, however, the plant closure meant they would actually be able to finish their education. They saw it as a gift. They knew they were not fulfilling their full potential at the plant. These were the assembly line workers of whom Studs Terkel said, "Most of us, like assembly line workers, have jobs that are too small for our spirit." These students could be picked out in the classroom. Their communication skills were comparable to what one would expect in any adult and, in some cases, comparable to the teacher. And even though they may have been fearful about their abilities when they came through the front door, they were "quick studies" when it came to teacher expectations. They were remarkable students embraced by the teachers, who shed tears when they left.

Even still, these students felt old and saw their age as a detriment. The adage "thirty and out" had been their escape hatch and their lifeline to retirement. Forty-year-old men and women, in plant terms, were old and, in many cases, physically wore out. Now, here they were—old, wore out, and without a job.

The Job Center: This Time Was Different

> There was a lot of disbelief that they were going to close the facility...there had been rumors; it was challenging to them. It was like grief for some of them.
>
> Case Manager, Rock County Job Center

Introduction

The new journey for GM and assembly line workers at other plants in 2008 was either to find another job or to gain new skills. They came through the front door of the Rock County Job Center wearing their emotions on their sleeves. Some were frantic, some angry. But mostly they were afraid. What would they do now that their lifelong employment was gone? Most did not know at that moment that they needed to reinvent themselves, much less that they were capable of such a task.

Even before they came to college, workers had to walk through a maze of meetings and events at the local job center, which houses services for both employers and people looking for employment. The Rock County Job Center is one of many in Wisconsin and a unit of the Southwest Workforce Development Board, a division of the Wisconsin Department of Workforce Development. Some of the workers had used the job center services before during previous layoffs, but they had never gone there to look for another job or determine their education and training options. For some, this stop had been a brief interlude in their long history of employment. Now, it was their lifeline.

These were the "dislocated" workers under federal law, defined as persons who have been terminated or laid off and are unlikely to return to a previous occupation, or persons whose prior place of employment has permanently closed or has laid off a large number of people. They were entitled to benefits. Some of the workers received benefits from the Workforce Investment Act (WIA) and some from the Trade Adjustment Assistance (TAA) program (what some students would call the "Cadillac" of benefits). The most fortunate workers had enough years to retire. Those who did not took severance payment, exercised their seniority rights and moved to plants in other cities such as Kansas City or Fort Wayne, or simply collected unemployment as long as they could. Others attempted to get another job. The only ones available were minimum wage jobs. Still others could afford to stay unemployed longer because they had 85 percent of their income in sub pay, and, at least initially, were able to use the GM Job Bank. The Job Bank allowed them to remain on the payroll and report to the union hall every day in case there was work. Over the course of two years, the Job Bank was eliminated. GM workers began showing up in larger numbers in 2009.

The First Challenges

The Job Services division of the Rock County Job Center employed case managers, and each of eleven case managers had about 175 workers on their case load. Orientations for the workers took place at the job center or, in the case of General Motors employees, the UAW hall. They were called Rapid Response Sessions. For those who wanted to go to college, they had to attend an orientation. Because there was so much paper work that had to be completed and many options, it was very confusing. When workers were asked what they signed up for, sometimes they had no idea. Color-coding was implemented:

> Workers would say, "OK, I want to get in." I would say, "Have you attended the orientation?" They didn't know. With the color-coding I could say, "How many blue folders do you have? If two, then you have had orientation." If they had any green paperwork, that was TAA, so we would know what they had done. We had to explain the process.
>
> Workers would say, "I think I signed up for something, but I don't know what." I would say, "Please

print." But they would write, and I couldn't read the name. That was something we asked, "Please, pay attention; you need to print your name. We try to contact you, and if we can't, we go on to the next name." Even that was a problem.

Case Manager

Emotions ran high. Case managers needed to be empathetic. Workers needed someone to listen to them other than people who were in the same boat. They had talked to each other enough. Many case managers could honestly advocate for the value of college, as they themselves were recipients of degrees and had seen their lives change. Some of them had been in poverty and received food stamps prior to getting a degree. These workers needed good advice and a good ear to help them decipher this new stage of their lives.

They thought being in their thirties was too old to go back to school. I said, "When I got my divorce, I was on welfare. It wasn't easy with a small child. When he got into kindergarten, I went to school. He's twenty-eight now." This was a scary experience that I shared that helped these folks.

I said, "I know, I didn't like school, but you have this opportunity that someone is going to pay for your education." I hired people from Lear and GM. They were familiar faces at the Job Center. It was easier then for them. Maybe this is something I should do. They needed a familiar face.

Case Manager

At first, there was anger and disbelief among the workers regarding their job loss. This was the most prominent sentiment, but not universal. Some workers saw this as their second chance. They hated their jobs as assembly line workers. This was their chance to go to college. It was their kick in the butt. This was just what they needed. They never were able to focus on a degree before, so this was a chance to focus. How can I go to school and how long will it take? What kind of funding?

Case Manager

The majority who came through, they were dependable and reliable. They said, "I haven't missed a day of work in ten years. But when I get sick, I get sick." They were proud. There were a few who had issues that were going to make it very difficult to find employment. We actually had an individual who tried to get into the program and his voicemail message was horrendous. For weeks, we said, "You have got to change that. Employers are going to say, 'He is going into the circular file!'" He finally changed his voicemail. Same thing with e-mail addresses; I got an e-mail from "sheep girl." I'm not quite sure what that means.

Case Manager

Understanding the Past Before Moving Forward

Some workers described to their case managers how they accidentally got into assembly line work in the beginning. They were just going to take the summer off out of high school before going to college and earn some good money. Then family obligations came along and, thirty years later, here they were with no degree, no discernible skills, and no job.

For others, there was never a question that they would go to the plant. Most of these workers said they had not enjoyed high school. They felt forced to sit in a classroom, found the lessons boring, and really thought college was going to be just like high school. Instead, they were told by the job center staff that they would be in classes that included hands-on skill experience. As each case manager talked about the value of college, they could see they were making some progress. Where, in the beginning, workers had dug in their heels with regard to not going to college, now their attitude began to change. In their technical skills classes, they were told, they could take things apart, put them back together, and diagnose problems. For those interested in health care, they would be practicing on each other taking blood pressure, for example, before they saw actual live patients at the hospital. They would be using computerized simulators to show them how actual patients would respond to medical events. This started to sound interesting.

Narrowing the Field

One of the next challenges was helping workers discover what new field would be a good fit for them. Most workers had had a "job" all their lives; they had no idea what a career was. This is where the aptitude test, Job Fit, came in. This three-hour test reviewed interest in occupations that require at least a two-year degree or less than a four-year degree. Many workers, however, were looking for a quicker educational experience than two years even. So, perhaps, a job like truck driving might work. But those workers over fifty-five years old did not think this career would work at their age.

Once they tested and received their assessments, the workers went online to see the job duties of a particular occupation. They researched whether it was a growing field or a shrinking field. Some workers did not want to go into the field suggested. While some knew what they wanted to do, others didn't have a clue. Never had they had to think about their future.

Former unionized workers told their caseworkers they wanted to go into occupations that had the approximate starting salary level of their former jobs, between twenty-one and twenty-six dollars per hour. A case manager had to explain reality:

> You are going to be an entry-level worker. You are not going to be able to make the same wages. If you think back, you had to work your way up. It sucks, but that's how it works.

Case managers also talked the workers through the realities of different occupations:

> With nursing, you have to be able to figure it out. You are still going to have to deal with people throwing up and having diarrhea. This is part of the process. You will clean up after accidents. If you can't handle this, we need to look at something else.

> With lower math scores, we suggested using the lab here. "We want to see you be successful. We don't want to see you fail." They said, "So, you care about what happens to me?" That seemed to make a difference to them.

Once they go off to college, they come back to us as case managers. They brag about those grades. "I made the dean's list." We love that! We get to live vicariously. Once they secure that first job, they are so excited. That's why we're here. It makes up for all of the grumpy people at the beginning.

But, once the workers went to college, both they and their case managers continued to struggle with acronyms and different processes. What was the difference between application, registration, and enrollment? Sometimes, students told their case managers they had enrolled when, in fact, they had applied and been accepted only. It became incumbent upon college personnel and caseworkers to have weekly meetings to sort out all of the misunderstandings. In this way, the caseworkers could better serve their clients. Just attempting to sort out benefits proved to be a bit of a nightmare for over seven hundred students, all attempting to start at once, but this situation emphasized the importance of having good, solid relationships between the agencies. With all of the inherent stressors in a situation such as this, people with sound minds and temperament were what the situation demanded. Luckily, these people existed in large measure at the job center and at the college.

Transitioning to Blackhawk Technical College

At first, I thought I was a victim.

Jim, Student

In the end, workers with a wide range of cognitive ability came to Blackhawk Technical College from the Rock County Job Center. Some students were able to hit the ground running, others needed coaxing and reassurance about their abilities, and some struggled with all their might. Was it the assembly line work that reinforced their deficits? Would those who struggled and needed much reassurance and hand-holding have exhibited these traits regardless of the nature of their previous work? Possibly. But it is doubtful that as a group they would have shown these traits in such great numbers and to such a degree.

When the new students arrived at the front door of the college, many had never stepped foot in an institution of higher education. Only one out of five had previous college credits, making the adjustment a little easier, but most had not been in a classroom since high school, had been below average students, and had memories of that experience as being unpleasurable. Although their case managers acted as cheerleaders, assuring them this experience would be different, they had no clue what to expect. Some never made it past the application process. In fact, out of approximately 5,183 who were out of work, only 1,500 enrolled at Blackhawk Technical College within two years of the plant closing.

Many of the new students were angry and frustrated. The frustration, some would later admit, masked their fear that they were not college material. Some had been told this all of their lives, and that assessment pushed them into the assembly plants, similar to generations before them. These stories speak of fear that they would be sitting next to students who were half their age who knew a lot about computers. Surely they would not be able to measure up to be "real" college students. And would they be able to stay committed for the length of time it would take to earn an important credential?

Students who came first were those who had no extended benefits to supplement their unemployment insurance benefits. Their financial situation was precarious. Some were not willing to scale down their standard of living, having gotten used to a previous income that was substantial. They spent what they earned, buying boats, snowmobiles, RVs, etc., and ended up with no savings to fall back on. Some had to live in their cars when they could no longer make their mortgage payments.

Older workers were extremely doubtful that anyone would want to hire them at the age of fifty-seven. They perceived there would be age discrimination. They really believed they had been in a train wreck and were powerless to change the circumstances. Some could not handle it. They went back to the Job Center. They couldn't wrap their minds around the major change that was happening in their lives. They couldn't believe they had the power to choose what they wanted to do with the rest of their lives. They simply did not have the emotional wherewithal to rally their families around this change. They still believed something would happen...perhaps the plant would open again. They dropped out.

A year later, they were back. They said they couldn't get a job, and the only way they would get benefits was to go to school. They were the unwilling participants, but they ultimately knew this would be the only way they might make more than minimum wage. One such student knew about computers and believed he had the skills to get a job in the information technology field. He didn't understand why he had to come to college to get a certificate. He wanted to get in and get out as quickly as possible. The certificate, the credential that required the fewest courses, was his way to do this.

People cannot attend college, generally speaking, unless they are a high school graduate or a recipient of a GED (General Education Diploma). Hundreds of workers among those who lost their jobs at GM and other plants had not finished high school or completed a GED. Where previously there was no sense of urgency, now the demand for GED completion skyrocketed. At least two hundred people signed up within a two-week period. For these students, the road ahead was longer and less certain.

Students who had the easiest time were those who had previous college credit. For these students, the plant closing was a gift. Now, they could go to college full time, have government benefits to pay tuition, and devote all of the time they previously spent at the plant to classes and homework. One such student took an early retirement, received her Associate of Applied Science Degree in Nursing, and is now a registered nurse.

If the students thought they had been tested and prodded and examined at the Job Center, they were in for more of the same at college. Almost all colleges use an entrance or placement test of some sort to determine the student's basic literacy skills: TABE (Test of Adult Basic Education) or the appropriate level for course placement (COMPASS). These tools place students where he or she belongs based on his or her skill level. The placement tests are designed for ninth- to twelfth-grade course levels, while the literacy tests measure fifth- to eighth-grade performance.

Some of the more rigorous programs at the college require a substantially higher placement score, so students who were enrolling in these programs had to do developmental or remedial work before they retest and attempt to get a higher score. Some of the less than degree-level programs do not require a particular Compass score, so students immediately started taking core courses in the program. In most community and technical colleges, however, 65 percent of all entering students, even those right out of high school, need to take at least one developmental or precollege course, usually math. Regardless of their proficiency, the workers were extremely anxious about taking the placement test. One described his emotional state at the time as "sweating bullets."

Two-thirds of the workers tested at the ninth- to twelfth-grade levels. Approximately one-third tested below the ninth grade level and had to brush up on their basic literacy skills. Not many of the workers tested below the fifth grade level, although there were some. These students had to be served by community organizations and literacy councils in the community. Overall, students did much better on their entrance exams than they thought they would. In many cases, they did better than recent high school graduates.

Once students took their placement tests, if they were lucky, they attended an orientation. In some cases, large group orientations were held at all times of the day and evening. These orientations included over two hundred students and were voluntary. However, because of the large numbers of students, not all students attended an orientation or met with a counselor or advisor. There simply were too many students and not enough help. This created problems because the language and terminology of the college was so different. Consistent with their experience of having behavior dictated to them at the plant, some thought the college selected classes for them.

When people came into the advisors' offices, some were looking for the money. They were asked what they really wanted to do and what would make them happy getting up every morning? One student who wanted to make comparable money to his GM hourly wouldn't take no for an answer. There are two or three program areas where entry-level pay is comparable to GM, those being in health sciences and robotics. This student chose nursing. The advisor asked if he was strong in either math or science; if he wasn't, these two fields would be challenging unless he was willing to spend considerably more than the two years of benefits he had. He insisted on nursing.

The student came back into the counseling center two weeks later because the math was too hard. He said he was ready to look at reality. He went into business management and continued to come in once or twice a week to make sure he was on the right path. He said he was not used to thinking and wanted to make sure his thought process was intact. He came into the counseling center to thank the advisor because he helped him go from the beginning with muddy thinking to clarity, and he knew he had come in with an air of arrogance. He is now at John Deere.

Students needed to put together a plan. Once they had a plan of action in place, some of the fear went away. For some, it took longer for the fear to go away:

He was on a library tour. His hands were shaking, his body, too. He was more nervous than the others. He was in his fifties and frail. He said he just didn't know if he could do this work. Over the course of time, there was a change. The shaking was gone, and he was getting As in his classes. When I saw him again in the halls, the transformation was apparent. When I saw him a third time at a Phi Theta Kappa function (the national honor society for community and technical colleges), I threw away the speech I was going to give to the new students and decided to use the transformation of this particular student as the basis of my speech. He was, after all, living testimony to the change that can occur in students from doubting Thomases to someone who can be a stellar student.

VP of Student Services,
Blackhawk Technical College

Immediate Challenges

I'm going to tell you right now. I know nothing about computers.

Student

The separation between thinking and doing the workers had experienced at the plant surfaced in many ways at the college. First, students themselves acknowledged that they "were just old factory workers." This phrase was repeated time and again to teachers in a plea for teachers not to expect too much from them. More than one teacher heard from students about the fact that thinking was hard, not to mention that computer use was new to many of these workers as well.

The Technology Tunnel

The gnashing of teeth could be heard clear across the campus. Then, the whining and tears began. The first week of classes had begun. The first homework assignments were given. Students were surprised they were expected to use word processing to turn in their homework.

The college was unprepared for the level of unpreparedness of most students when it came to computer use, particularly, word processing. The fact that these students had been living in a "technology tunnel" became apparent immediately. Most students previously had no need to use a computer, but technology use is a core competency for students as well as workers today. Students simply cannot be a student today without knowledge of how to use a computer beyond the Internet. The college held the line. The struggle was on.

> I remember that first day, and I wanted them to become familiar with e-mail. I asked them to send me an e-mail. One said, "This is my first e-mail. It took me all morning." The majority had very few skills. I had been surrounded by people with computer skills. I thought any job would have required a computer. I was wrong.
>
> Teacher

Mark was one of those students whose previous jobs did not require a computer. He said computers frightened him and he "had never turned one on." He learned:

> We had classes on computers and about computers, as far as input and output. There was a

big difference in my confidence level after a time. My brother came from England. He saw me using the computer and he said he wanted to cry when I was opening all of those Windows. We also had keyboard classes. We had to pass the class. We had to get twenty words per minute. I got up to twenty-four words per minute.

Mark was fortunate to have been in a class where students take all of their courses together, and they were in class twenty hours a week. Most students in that class struggled with computers, so he was not alone. Other workers who came to Blackhawk were placed in regular courses. This transition was more difficult. From day three of the semester, it became apparent something had to be done. Students were not going to be successful in any of their courses if they could not use word processing and e-mail at a minimum. One student learned this the first day of her business class. The teacher was explaining what to expect in the class. He said, "You will be required to do a Power Point presentation." She raised her hand, "What's a Power Point?"

In order to get students help quickly, college administrators set up one-on-one tutoring for students around the lunch hour. All instructors and students were informed that such tutoring would be available. Also, more basic computer courses were added to the schedule and more courses were added at the Job Center. The problem with the additional classes for students was the schedules. They already had their schedules in place, and they could not add any additional class time.

By far, the most successful response to the problem was the one-on-one tutoring between staff and students. Everyone at the college pitched in, including members of the President's Cabinet. The chief information officer set up additional times for students to set up their college e-mail accounts, but their needs were so much more basic than that:

My student's name was Jeff. I asked him if he needed help setting up a Word document for a paper. He said, "I don't even know how to use a computer. I don't even know how to turn it on." He had worked at Lear Seating. He was forty-six years old. He knew he had to learn. It was three weeks into the semester, and he had a paper due. I said, "Here's the different software." We started at the very beginning. I showed him the functionality, opening up a document, and saving a document. He had some questions. We spent thirty-five or forty minutes just going through some basic functions.

Member of the President's Cabinet

This cabinet member occasionally saw Jeff throughout the remainder of the fall semester when they passed in the hall. In the spring semester, he was invited into a supervisory leadership classroom along with other college supervisors to evaluate the quality of student group final presentations. To his surprise Jeff was a part of one group:

Their presentation included a business plan for a company they set up, plus a product they developed and would market, etc. They included how they would operationalize the plan. There were four students in Jeff's group. Although Jeff probably didn't put together the PowerPoint, he was using the remote mouse to advance the slides and discussing items on the page. He had a level of comfort in doing so. Clearly, this was not exceptional, but it was pretty rewarding to see someone who did not know how to use a computer, a factory worker, who now was part of the group, performing with a level of professionalism and confidence. I was impressed.

Some of the long-term solutions for future students were put into place at the earliest possible opportunity. At the very next semester group orientation, attended by more than two hundred students, announcements were made about the availability of computer tutoring and additional classes. Actually, this second round of students had heard from their friends who came before them about the problems with using computers, so they had taken this to heart and registered for a computer class they thought would teach them computer basics. The title of the course they had registered for was Intro to MS Office Suites. They thought that this "introduction" was a beginning course in using computers. Unfortunately, college staff did not find out how these students had taken the bull by the horns and made their own selection of a computer class until after classes started. This was not a basic computer course.

Thus, a second round of teeth gnashing began. This time, students arrived in the counselors' offices stating they were lost in the first week because their instructor was talking about Excel and Word and students did not have a clue what these were. So, they had to drop the class and try to get into another class more appropriate to their skill level.

At the very next orientation, college staff came with drop slips and a list of computer classes, starting with the basic class. Students who had pre-registered for the Intro to MS Office Suites course were told to stay after the orientation and complete a drop and add slip. Many complied.

Not all assembly line workers identified themselves as needing a basic computer class. Some indicated to admissions staff at the time of placement testing that they, in fact, did know how to use a computer. They were taken at their word and registered for classes. Only there was a problem. They really didn't know how to use computers. They had surfed the Internet. They may even have sent an e-mail. Certainly, they were far ahead of some of their peers, but they didn't know what Word was, nor had they ever used any form of word processing. So, here was another angle of the "technology tunnel" that blindsided college staff. How do you know exactly what computer skills the students really, honestly, possess?

The final round of efforts to attack the problem was the development of a check-off list for students to complete at the time they took their other preliminary testing during admission. Students self-reported exactly what programs they had used in the past. This was by far the best way to help students and staff members see the deficiencies. Basic keyboard skills were added to the mix of classes offered, but it took one year to convince the funding agency to pay for these basic courses. Never before in their funding discussions had these deficiencies come to their attention, but the need was so great that additional resources were expended toward this effort.

Age, Image, and Self-Esteem

Self-esteem can come only from earning your own reward.

Peter Buffett, Life is What You Make It

But you don't understand, I'm just an old factory woman.

Student

The above plea for understanding was made to a communications instructor. It was in response to the first assignment that involved a short research paper. The student was asking the instructor to take pity on her and not have such a high expectation that she could do this assignment. This one statement said it all. This group of students was so fearful that they were not capable of doing assignments, and especially could not do the dreaded writing required of them, that they wanted to be excused. It didn't work. Their plea fell on deaf ears.

By far, the biggest concern of students was their ability to be a good student. Some wondered aloud how far behind their thinking processes were in relation to other students. They used the terms "rusty," "dusty," and "filled with cob webs" to describe the condition of their brain. Their worries were based on fear, not fact.

> The teachers in the program were wonderful.
> They didn't treat us like dummies. They didn't talk
> down to us.
>
> Student

When you know how the community sees you, whether you believe it or not, it can infiltrate your thinking. Students who worked in the plants believed that they were not valued in the community. They knew that some community members thought they were spoiled because they were earning too much money given their skill level. They were earning a high hourly wage. Most workers who came to the college were earning more than their instructors, who had substantially more education than they did. And, while workers at the plant made substantial contributions to not only the economic vitality of the community but to the cultural and charitable needs as well, they were still seen as "plant rats."

Students said it was important to them to prove that they were more than just plant rats, to prove that they were smart and good learners. One group of such students was in the Human Resources associate degree program. When they first came to the college, they were not sure they were going to get a fair shake because of the way they were seen in the community. They didn't know if college staff and faculty would feel the same way. Over time, they became so upbeat about the fact that they had "earned" the right to be honor students and the fact that this might come as a surprise to many in the community. They said it was not only important to them, but to their kids. They were smart…imagine that.

Age also played a big role for this group of students. Primarily, they thought they surely wouldn't feel comfortable at college because of their age. Many were in their early forties.

> It took a load off of my shoulders when I saw the
> other older students.
>
> Student

This particular student thought that her group of licensed practical nursing (LPN) students were getting more hours of instruction in theory courses compared to regular associate degree nursing (ADN) students because of their age. Little did she know that all LPN students, regardless of age, get twice as many theory hours in the classroom as ADN students. The student's mistaken belief that they were given more time because of their age certainly affirmed her belief that teaching older students must have been harder.

Who gets to define "old," though? In higher education, a review of publications refers to an adult student as anyone over the age of twenty-five. So, does forty-five tip the scale? Are they then considered really old students? Assembly line workers thought so.

What is the expectation instructors should have of students with barely concealed gray hair? Should it be any different than for students with pink hair? Should it be different for students who saw themselves as old or for students who had not stepped foot into a higher education institution in twenty to thirty years, if ever? instructors held the line and a lot of hands, asking students, "Repeat after me: I can do this." Many thought they would be embarrassed in the classroom. One said he was surprised at how much more seriously the older students took their studies than the younger students. He felt the younger students should be setting the pace, but they weren't. The same student believed that coming to college and having it paid for by the government was "like winning the lottery." Most of the older students were much more likely than the younger students to really see the benefit of going back to school, and they actually told the younger students as much. Not that the younger students always appreciated being told this. In fact, some younger students did not stick around once "the sea of gray hairs" showed up. One grandmother told the story about her granddaughter. She had started at the college in the fall semester. She left shortly after the semester started because she wanted "a real college experience." She did not want to go to college with people who were her parents' age. It was a drag, she said.

Age was compounded even further when it played a role related to students' multiple responsibilities as a parent, a spouse, and a student, with their student role often getting the short end of the stick. They struggled with time management. They tired more easily from hours upon hours of studying.

Their motivation to complete their studies was different than younger students, too. There is a phenomenon in higher education called a "ghost student." This describes a student who will be here today and gone tomorrow. The ghost student is a disappearing student. No matter what class, it is a given that students will disappear, and teachers never know why. But the assembly line workers did not disappear. In the beginning, many thought they would just go to school until they found a job or they changed their mind. Instead, they no longer looked for a job and became committed students.

In fact, some got pretty comfortable in this environment. One instructor described a situation with her class where the students would come to class early with their thermos of coffee, rearrange the chairs, and have a coffee chat before the class started. They were attempting to duplicate their work environment at the plant. The instructor would stick her head around the corner at the entrance of the classroom and ask if it was time for her to come in yet. Both students and teacher laughed at this turn of events.

On a few rare occasions, a student's obvious age and attitude got in the way, but these were the exceptions. One plant worker in her sixties came to the supervisor of the general education division with a transcript in hand from the 1970s. She wanted to be assured that her written communications course would transfer into the college. She was told that the course she had taken did not include the use of computers. In any associate degree program, she would be required to take a writing class in which she used computers.

She argued with the supervisor and told her that she could not use a computer and she never would. She "didn't believe in them." The dean assured her that she might not know how to use a computer yet, but there were many ways to get help with her computer skills and this competency was one all employers required for most jobs. She became irate and told the dean that she was standing between her and her new career. She stated that the dean's refusal to allow the transfer of this course meant that the student would lose her house and she would have to live under a bridge.

The Classroom: Foreign Territory or Meaningful Assignments

What students bring into the classroom has more to do with their past than with the future or even the present. There are no blank slates. In some cases, the slates on which we chalk our lessons are severely fractured. But, at our best, teachers have the power to alter students' histories, if only in small ways.

Jeff VandeZande, "Close Encounters," *Chronicle of Higher Education*

Assembly line culture did not lend itself to the college classroom. At the plant, there were bells and whistles that signal a break, lunch, and end of shift. If you had to go to the bathroom, you had to find someone to take your place. The entire ten-hour day is highly regulated by sounds and equipment noise. Communication with other line workers is not encouraged nor is it physically possible.

In college, there are no bells to tell you when to do anything. Students can go to the restroom when the need arises, and they are encouraged to communicate with their instructors regularly. They are encouraged to raise their hand when they have a question. This freedom was foreign to these students, and it took a while for them to get comfortable with it.

While students became acclimated with their freedoms and due process rights, at times they were not enamored with the concept of academic freedom in the classroom. Some students fell back on their union background, and in times of conflict with the instructor, they treated the dean of the division like their union steward, there to "fix" the situation with the instructor. The fact that instructors are given enormous leeway to manage their classrooms and to teach their way was not what students wanted to hear. Nevertheless, instructors tried their best to make students feel comfortable, and the students did their best to be good students.

> Now we're seeing the older students from the
> GM dislocation, and they are heart-attack serious
> about school. This is their chance and they're go-
> ing to take full advantage of their chance and get it
> while the getting's good, so to speak.
>
> Steve, Instructor

"We can create an environment that nurtures the brain," states James Zull in *The Art of Changing the Brain.* The way to do this is by creating an environment in the classroom where students are not afraid to ask questions. The second most important part of the classroom environment is to build learning around what students already know and has meaning for them.

Steve knew this. He had created and taught a course on student success for several years, and ethics and economics for fifteen years. He was a well-liked. There were several ways he reeled students in with discussions centered on things they knew. Some of his examples to explain a principle or concept were related to raising kids and maintaining relationships. Since many people had these, they could relate.

43

He taught a section in economics on how it pays to go to school, called "opportunity cost." The students compared their lives and their choices between two paths: go to college or work in a factory. While in the past he had younger students in class who hadn't worked much yet, with the plant workers, the discussion was "quite robust." They talked about their regret in not going to college right out of high school. Steve asked the students, "Who did not make the most of their high school educational experience?" Over 90 percent admitted that was the case. They realized taking high school more seriously would have made going to college much easier.

Another assignment in economics related to the conditions of employment. Many younger students had "pie in the sky" ideas about benevolent employers. It used to surprise those students when Steve announced "their employers didn't care about them." Not anymore. When he talked about this with former plant workers in class, "it unleashed the floodgates of complaints," as the dislocated plant workers were living proof of this fact.

One of Steve's students was a plant manager with no education beyond high school. He was a very smart and reasonable guy. He was simply fascinated with the academic foundational ideas of what he essentially had been practicing for many years as a supervisor.

It would not surprise anyone that managers and line workers had different perspectives they brought with them into the classroom. There were conflicts and tension. In one section of Steve's class, he split teams into managers and employees. The employees say managers are a bunch of people who don't want to listen. Then, the employees switch sides and become managers. Steve spoke of this as a "teachable moment," where students get to know what the other side is thinking. He even had the class develop a management and union contract. Students had a lot of fun, and it built empathy about other people and their roles. This knowledge was vital to future employment situations.

From Economics to the Laboratory

Harry also knew you had to use examples and analogies with students that had meaning for them. Unlike Steve, Harry had been teaching laboratory sciences for only one year. His job in the one-year diploma program was to prepare students for future science courses where they would have to conduct laboratory skills with precision.

Harry knew there would be a gap in connecting science, lab work, and precision. He needed a concept and exercise that students could identify as part of their life experience. So, he decided that the concept of a recipe was an analogy he could use because most people would be familiar with it in the home. He decided that the class would make bread. He used scales, calibrated instruments to weigh ingredients, but he didn't tell them what the outcome was. They weighed salt, yeast, and sugar. They ended up with bread, and he used a bread-making machine so that they pushed buttons. A good day was described as one where there was a "spark." When this happens, instructors are able to have a good discussion and get to the main idea. Then, the students can take what they already know and go to the next level of learning.

Harry and his colleague Sue both knew that students learn at their own speed. Often, it was not until the advanced courses that students realized how this all fits together. Before they would ask, not unlike other students, "Why do I need this?" Now, they saw how all of the courses relate to their future job in the labor force. The instructors worked as a team. Harry knew where every student was in terms of his or her understanding of the material. Sue knew students had to learn to trust her.

Interpersonal and "Soft" Skills

In line with other teachers' concerns about communication skills of these students, Harry and Sue knew this was still a deficient skill area. Students took courses in written communications and technical report writing. They also took oral communications courses. But both teachers knew that in some cases this was not nearly enough. Students were going to be working with people in a health care environment who had more education than themselves and who had chosen this field as a career. At times, their lack of proper English was evident and their communication style could be described as "rough."

When You Begin Way Behind the Eight Ball: Adult Basic Education

> I never told my kids I had not graduated from
> high school.
>
> Melissa, Student

Now Melissa would have to. She had kept this secret from her kids because she wanted them to go to college. She had always stressed the importance of education to them. She knew she would have to go back to school to get her GED. When she told them, they were surprised. They assumed because she stressed to them the importance of completing their high school education that she had done so.

So started Melissa's journey back to school to take GED instruction and take her exams. Though she struggled with math, she became a model student. She ended up giving the GED graduation speech.

> My hands were shaking. I didn't know there were
> going to be so many people. I broke down and cried
> when I got my diploma in the mail.
>
> Some people thought that after I got my GED,
> I should seek any full-time job. But I knew better. I
> said, "This college learning is not that hard."

Melissa represented a group of students who came to Blackhawk without high school credentials. Approximately five hundred workers who came out of the plants were in this position. For these students the road was tougher and required a higher level of motivation. When you add middle age and low self-esteem to the mix, those who taught them also had a tougher challenge. But, tough, experienced, and passionate the instructors were.

The Unsung Heroes

Adult Basic Education (ABE) teachers teach the lowest level of literacy skills to adults. They are the unsung heroes of community and technical colleges because their task is great, and their rewards and the impact on society is enormous.

The Wisconsin Technical College system is fortunate to have adult basic education instruction within technical colleges. Other state systems locate ABE in K-12 or in the Department of Workforce Development. The value of having it in two-year colleges is that it is housed under the same umbrella as other college instruction. With instructors at all levels at the same table, it is easier to see curriculum gaps and needed skill alignments.

Some assembly line workers who tested at lower literacy levels became part of a repositioning bridge program known as the Career and Technical Education (CATE) program. This program was developed and implemented with financial resources from Senator Herb Kohl, then Chairman of the Senate Appropriations Committee. These students tested between sixth and ninth grade on their literacy skills. Some became eligible simply because they were dislocated and needed computer skills and refresher student success instruction.

All students had to self-select one of three occupational programs of interest: business, nurse assistant, or welding. After one semester of basic skills in computers, reading, writing, and math, as well as a student success course, they transitioned into credit classes for their respective occupational areas, where basic skills instructors still supplemented their occupational instruction. Students received approximately ten credits over two semesters. Once students completed these two semesters, they continued on with their respective career pathways. Completion rates in these programs were 50 percent higher than for regular program students.

"Initially, you have to assure them that they are capable of doing this work," said instructor Sheila. "They looked like deer in the headlights, and overall, they just did not know if they were cut out for all of this." In a new student success class, a course developed just in time for the plant workers, they wrote about their fears. This seemed to help them get over the hump. Melissa loved the student success course:

> One of the assignments was to outline our goals on a dream board. On the board I made a huge flower with eight petals. My first goal was the GED, so I colored in the petal. The next was work-based learning, so I colored in another petal. The third petal was taking business administration classes. Then, the last petal is receipt of an administrative professional degree. I look at this board and I say, I continue to accomplish a lot!

Melissa thought she was old (forty-one) and, not unlike the other plant workers, worried that she would be the oldest student in the class.

> I felt better when I came into the classroom and saw that I wasn't the oldest student. I didn't miss one day. There were younger students, but they dropped out. One dropped after one week. It just amazed me that they did that. This was such a great opportunity.

Skill Deficits

In addition to basic literacy skills, these students needed basic computer skills. Just getting students comfortable using a computer was the first task.

> I had them play a game of solitaire, and they had to use a mouse without getting too frustrated. They start with the basics: using a keyboard, using a mouse,

and understanding terminology (e.g., what is a moni-

tor, what is a network). They needed to know hard-

ware and software.

Sheila

In addition to basic computer use, there were also sometimes severe deficits in writing and language use. There was a lot of conversation in the classroom, so Sheila could see where the students were in terms of their skill level. There was definitely a lot of slang used and sometimes a little profanity.

I would coach them. When I told them this lan-

guage was not appropriate, they would say, "Are you

serious?" Some didn't know any better. We talked

about vernacular, using such words as "ain't" and

"jus" and "wanna," and they don't know that this

is not appropriate. As far as they were concerned,

it was OK on the assembly floor. Also, one of the

biggest challenges is that the writing is horribly low.

These are people who struggle to write 500 words.

Sheila

Making Progress

The change in these basic skills students was the most profound, starting from the first week when they came in fearful, and progressing to the second week when they relaxed. The group arrangement was beneficial, too. Having them in a group of students all in the same boat was a tremendous plus.

These students come in strangers and by the end

of the term they were planning vacations together,

giving rides to each other, going fishing together.

49

And they weren't very shy about calling people on the carpet because of their absences. It's an accountability thing. They know each other and they know there will be days when you will not want to show up and the others will pull you through. So, I really think they needed each other.

After the first semester, they knew each other, and in new classes they set up the seating arrangements and tended to hang with people they had known from the first semester. This support for each other eliminated a lot of fear. It functioned almost like a support group.

Sheila, Instructor

Changing Cultures: From Blue Collar to White Lab Coat

I would have been kicking their asses, had I not left (the classroom).

Student

For some new students, conflict resolution skills did not exist. College administrators and instructors did not know this. They do now. In the case of the student quoted above, the administrator whose job it was to resolve the conflict in that classroom was caught off guard.

Mary is an administrator in the health sciences programs at the college and had not had this much of a blue-collar experience before. She says she had been "cloistered." Her mother was an artist and a piano teacher, and her father was a teacher. She was not all that different from most nursing instructors in community and technical colleges. The majority had a middle class background, and all had two university degrees. Their exposure to and intermingling with other socioeconomic groups was limited to the classroom. While she had a lot of cultural diversity in her background, she did not have much experience with the culture she was witnessing.

While all of the workers from the plant were making middle class wages, in some cases more than the instructors, not all had come from homes where good communications skills were taught. For those who came from a culture of poverty and had been a plant worker all their lives, behaviors and communication style could clash with classroom expectations. This was particularly true when it came to conflict resolution.

> The environment they were in did not require them to work out conflict. They did not have to take responsibility for conflict over all those years. When the rubber met the road, they were not forced to work things out.
>
> Mary, Administrator

Several differences between plant culture and expectations for future health services employees quickly became apparent. In health care, an employee's ability to work in teams and resolve their own conflict with other employees is expected. This is not unique to health care by any means, as most employers expect their employees to resolve their own conflicts with coworkers. However, at the plant, if workers had a complaint against one another, they took it to the union steward. They would have others resolve their conflicts. In all likelihood, some students who came from this environment simply never had to learn these skills. They came to the college still looking for others to resolve these situations.

Differences of these kinds were more pronounced in classrooms where all students were former plant workers. Several of these classes were for health care occupations. Factions caused significant divisions in classrooms; there was drama, and there were cliques. Sometimes there was intra-plant discord. While these problems got resolved over time, they initially distracted from the core mission of the class. Administrators had to explain what the college's and the profession's expectations were.

> I've seen a tremendous difference in the class, and I think it has to do with the difference of factory culture, belonging to a strong union that has a lot of detail spelled out in roles and function. We talk about what the academic culture and culture of health care will be like and how they're really going to have to make this transition…and, I'm hoping, making them aware is addressing their needs.
>
> Mary, Administrator

Student Expectations and Performance

Linda taught two groups of students, primarily from the plants, in the licensed practical nursing program. Most would make the transition to become registered nurses.

> Their reading skills and their overall academic skills were strong. Even to have gotten this far was good. Two of the students had previously been at Blackhawk and found out they knew each other. They said they would not have been successful twenty years ago. Life issues got in the way too much. They finished together.
>
> Linda

> But, there were challenges. In the beginning, everything had to be exactly the same. These nursing students needed to believe they were all being treated equally, even when it came to the patients they were taking care of at their hospital clinical sites. There was the real idea of equal versus fair, which may have come from all plant workers under union contract needing to be treated fairly on the line.
>
> Linda

The problem was they were dealing with patients in the hospital, not automotive parts, with each one having a very different set of circumstances. Students complained because they believed the instructor was not grading each student-patient encounter fairly. Of course, each student-patient encounter would be entirely different because of the specifics of the patient's condition. Students also complained that the instructor was spending more time with one student over another. They were extremely competitive.

Instructor Expectations

One of the other skill areas that elicited lots of stress was critical thinking. In the world of the plant, pieces that came down the line were either good or not. Thinking centered on things that were "either/or" but not both. In nursing, there is a lot of gray area.

> I worked a lot on critical thinking totally unrelated to nursing. We did a lot of gaming things to get them to think differently in general. In their former world, they were not encouraged to think outside of the box.
>
> Linda

Developing critical thinking and oral communication skills required a lot of role playing. They had to interview each other using scenarios about acute care or hospital circumstances. They had to create different scenarios, like sitting with loved ones when a patient was being resuscitated. In some of the roles, they were stumped and silent. They did not know what to say in life-and-death scenarios. The instructor had to model the appropriate behavior back to them.

> I tell them, "You have already been a success. You
>
> got through the door, through registration process,
>
> got through your general education courses, so you
>
> have already done these things." They adapt pretty
>
> quickly. They find that they really like it. They like
>
> the freedom, they like the imagination, and they
>
> have not done much of this before.
>
> Linda

Most of these students had the cognitive ability to be successful. They studied in groups in the laboratory all the time. This was quite different than regular students. These students did not have to be told to study. Perhaps, instructors thought, the bonding among them was greater because of their similar backgrounds. And, there were some pretty dramatic changes in individual behavior.

> I saw one loud and dominating student who was
>
> told to cool her jets by the other students. Her be-
>
> havior got modified. That was a good thing. She was
>
> rubbing people the wrong way.
>
> Administrator

In the end, they were very good students and had great success on their licensure exam.

> This was a different type of student. In both LPN
> groups, we only lost three or four compared to ten. I
> think they dealt with this better than our traditional
> students. These students were well-established and
> had clear, concrete goals.
>
> Linda

Susan was one of them. She had worked at Lear Seating, a plant that supplied seats for the GM SUVs, for over a decade. She was determined to finish this time. This was her third time in college.

> I came here right out of high school in 1990. I
> came again in 1999 when I was laid off, but I got
> called back. I was a single mom. I had to pick my
> battles. I had no other income. I did work in nurse
> assistant jobs every other weekend.
>
> Susan

Susan married someone from the plant, and they had two children, one in 2003 and one in 2005. Her husband had been a Blackhawk student as well. To say that she hated her job would be an understatement. What she hated was the environment.

> Mainly the morale on the line, the whole atmo-
> sphere. But, most of the time, I hated going to work.
> It was very boring. Ten-hour shifts doing the same
> old thing.
>
> Susan

By the time the plant closed, she had all of her prerequisite courses completed and was in "program ready" status. One of the things that she loved about coming to Blackhawk was seeing so many others she knew:

> It was like a mini-Lear here. You turned the corner and see about five people. It was kind of nice. Everyone had the same goals. Some of the others might have been scared. I was excited.

When asked what challenged her the most, Susan said:

> If I didn't have the two little children and the finances, I would have been fine. The time commitment and time management—those were the main things. It wasn't the homework.

New Teachers, Angry Students

> I don't believe you can teach me anything!
> Industrial Maintenance Student

Not all interactions and exchanges between students and instructors went well. In fact, sometimes things got downright ugly, leading to meltdowns by instructors themselves. This was especially true with new young instructors, though some were closer in age to the students but still new to the teaching profession. Overall, these new instructors were not prepared for the level of animosity directed at them by people whose lives had been upended. Such was the case with Norm, a new instructor with twenty-five years of manufacturing experience.

Norm taught industrial maintenance, a one-year diploma program in which students learn repair processes for major manufacturing equipment. He was one of twenty-one limited-term instructors brought into the college because of the massive enrollment increase. He had four days to develop lesson plans.

> The first day of class was something else. I had no idea what I was dealing with. I told them we're both in this new endeavor, you as a new student after thirty years and me as a new teacher. I explained that patience would be tried on both ends. I said if there was an answer I didn't know, I would find it. I held true to that. One thing I remember is that I always used the word "we" and not "I" and that we were in this together.

One of Norm's students said, "I've been a machinist for thirty years, and you can't teach me anything." There were actually many things the student did not know. Company journeymen, regardless of company, had a much more limited set of skills than trade journeymen who are licensed by the state. Unfortunately, they did not know this until they lost their jobs and attempted to get jobs on the outside. They were extremely unhappy and angry about discovering these shortcomings after they left the plant.

In addition to students who thought they knew the trades, Norm also had some students who had no skills because they had worked the assembly line exclusively all of their lives.

> There would be times when they would be sitting there (in the classroom), and there was a point where I was going too fast. They looked like deer in the headlights. I asked if we needed to slow down. They all said, "Yes." They were intimidated by the

pace. We finally clicked, and we became a cohesive group.

One of the ways the group became cohesive was that they started helping each other. Norm intuitively knew that in order to keep the good students from getting bored as a result of a slower pace in class, he had to keep them involved in sharing their knowledge with those students who were struggling. Although Norm had no previous classroom experience, he had the good sense to co-opt the stronger students into a helping role. It worked well, and the formerly angry journeymen became teacher aides. Not only did this work with classroom management, these stronger students told Norm how much they liked that role. Who knew they would like teaching? In the end, the former angry students apologized for their behavior toward Norm.

Baptism by Fire for Younger Teachers

You are younger than my kids! What are they doing? Pulling you off the street just to have a teacher in the classroom?

Student

Pat was thirty-one and had an entirely different set of problems. She had been a medical assistant for eight years in various departments at a well-established local clinic. She knew her stuff, but she was inexperienced in the classroom. From the first day, things did not go well. She lectured from the book, issued a study guide with questions for purposes of studying for the tests, and told students that everything on the test would come from those questions on the study guide.

Unfortunately, correct answers to the study guide questions were not discussed before the first exam. The results of the test revealed that students had been answering the study guide questions wrong. Because the questions and answers were not discussed before the test, however, students did not know this. All hell broke loose when the test scores were revealed.

Pat went to her dean. The dean came into the classroom and talked to the students about the fact that Pat was a new instructor. She also spent more time with Pat talking about teaching technique. She told her that everyone who stands in front of the classroom has really bad days like this, even the most experienced instructors. This one incident did not mean she would be a failure as a teacher. She should chalk it up to a lesson learned and go back into the classroom with a renewed sense of purpose. She did. The rest of the semester went much more smoothly. Well, almost.

This particular group of students Pat taught took all of their classes together. They would be a tough audience under any circumstances, but particularly so for a new teacher who was not self-assured. Some of the students knew each other from the plant, so they sat together. Another group of students from another company sat together. Verbal skirmishes broke out between the groups when one group thought Pat was siding with the other group. Pat was told she needed to be more assertive and not let students change her mind. This was good advice that Pat took to heart.

One Year Later: Last Ditch Effort Prolongs Hope

Some of the workers believed the plant closing was temporary. Surely it would open again, just as it had before. This was just a temporary blip on their radar screen. Some workers thought management was just trying to get the older, higher-paid workers to retire.

This hope of reopening was kept alive by a yearlong effort of key individuals in the community, state, and federal government to persuade GM to reopen the plant. State and federal Democratic and Republican figures were involved. The effort failed. No matter how much laid off workers wanted to believe they would be going back to work at the plant, it soon became clear that, at least in the foreseeable future, this was not going to happen. The Janesville plant is the only one in the General Motors inventory that is still on standby.

The Road Less Travelled: Walking Away from General Motors

> A lot of them never had to think of what to do
> with their lives.
>
> Mike, Instructor

Intergenerational Communications

"I think the motivation depends on the maturity of the person," Mike said. "These are long-term Lear or GM people. This is an opportunity for them to reinvent themselves." Some took Mike up on reinvention, others did not. But Mike knew that, too. He had been teaching adult students for the last twenty years, primarily from manufacturing environments. "The class never gets stale. It's always something different, and the challenges are always there."

Mike taught leadership development and human resources courses. When he made team assignments, he made a point of putting older students with younger students.

> The younger student has the technology and the
> life experience of the older student go pretty well,
> and they feed off of each other's experience. The
> older student does the research and the younger
> student does the technology.

During a semester in one of Mike's classes, the assignment hit home for the older students and actually exemplified the differences in their life experiences. This particular class exercise was on employee compensation, and he splits the class into groups, and tries to make sure groups are age mixed. One student gets assigned the role of an employee getting a raise. Discussions play out just as they do in real life, with the young employee looking at "what's in it for me today," whereas the older students were looking at the long-term implications of giving raises. Younger students saw how these decisions are actually made as some of the older students had been involved in wage negotiations in their job. It was a teachable moment for them.

It was a fluke that Zeke was in Mike's class. He took it while he was waiting to get into the clinical nursing courses. It was apparent from the start that Zeke was a pretty highly motivated student. While many workers waited until the last minute to come to college, Zeke didn't. GM announced their plant closure during the spring of 2008, at first indicating they were going to close in 2010. That timing accelerated. They ended up stopping the line for GM automobiles in December 2008. Zeke began taking classes during the fall semester of 2008, before the plant closed. He took three courses in the evening, while still working the line during the day. His coworkers told him he was crazy for doing this.

His options at the time of the GM closure were that he could transfer to Fort Wayne, Indiana, or take a buy-out. He was thirty-nine, a single dad, and a widower. His children, adolescents and teenagers, had been through enough trauma when their mother died, and he did not want to uproot them. So, he chose the buy-out. He describes his feelings at the time.

> Honestly, my job loss was not that big of a deal. I said to my kids, "Dad will get a job here. We are going to stay here." Then, you go down to sign your papers giving up your transfer rights. There were only thirty of us. I knew what kind of money I was turning down. You are losing twenty-five to thirty dollars an hour. If you are hardworking, you can find a job. My income is substantially lower, of course.
>
> Zeke

Zeke had been in the US Navy and had worked at GM for thirteen years. He had no previous college credits.

Coming to Blackhawk was pretty scary at first. I went to the Learning Lab and got on the computers, using the programs there to help tutor me. I was originally in health sciences, but I had to improve my scores in math and science. It took me two to three weeks to get comfortable. I adjusted pretty well. I made the honor roll.

One of the assignments Mike gave his leadership development students was to create a personal vision statement that included core values. Zeke had never done anything close to this before. Mike then asked his students these questions: "Why are you here? What do you want out of life? What do you have a passion for?" Zeke was stumped. "I looked at the question for two days. No one had ever asked me that question before," he says.

He came back to class with his answer—his own business plan for a travel agency. He knew he always enjoyed travel, and he learned from his nurse assistant work that he really enjoyed people. He took a marketing class where he learned to do radio spots, and he started his business. He schedules twenty-five trips a year and does two to three big group trips in the region. At last word, he was venturing out internationally and planning trips in Europe.

Zeke now knows how different his life would have been had he not made the difficult choice of leaving GM. He credits his instructor with making his new career happen for him:

If it wasn't for Mike, I would have never had the courage to do this. Mike really changed my life.

Outside the Classroom: Students as Parents and Impact on Children

As blue-collar jobs disappear and strong relationships between postsecondary education and income grow, individuals in the United States are increasingly polarized into families with both high parental education and income, and families with neither…This counters the American promise of intergenerational mobility. Interventions that provide postsecondary access for parents promote intergenerational mobility for their children.

Don Peck, *Pinched*

It lit a fire underneath them. I showed them my transcripts with As. I told them, "See what can happen when you get your stuff done."

A student talking to his children

Every student who was a parent described the impact of college attendance on their children. The consequence of the parents doing homework was that their children saw them struggling and putting in the time. Parents thought this was important. They actually paid more attention to their children's academic performance, much to the children's dismay. In one case, the parent was no longer satisfied with his children receiving Cs. In another case, the child who had always gotten away with underperforming was not able to do so any longer. Children worked harder. Whether this sharing experience will have long-term impact is unknown, but at least for two or three years, their school performance was under the microscope.

Parents became very innovative in attending to their family obligations. One sat in the bleachers at a basketball tournament game doing homework. Other parents now irritated their children by competing for time on the home computer. In another case, a student who was taking chemistry had a child who was also taking chemistry. She was able to tell her child how things work. In another, both were using the same textbook. The kitchen table became the place where parent and child gathered after dinner. It became a bonding experience.

One student attended college along with his daughter. They did homework together. In fact, they both marched across the stage at graduation. The father said, "I don't think she would have been there had I not been there." Experiences such as these between parent and child may have a longer-lasting impact than people realize. Because the parent now has had college experience as well, discussions and dialogue between two generations merge into one shared experience. While this interaction has occurred for generations with one group of Americans, the new experience of these parents as students may again secure the promise of intergenerational mobility that is the heart of a secure middle class.

Part II – The Community College: Traditional Education Programs

The Place: Greenville, Michigan
The Plant: Electrolux
The College: Montcalm Community College

The voice over the phone was grim. "Governor, I have some troubling news. We've got another crisis. Electrolux is threatening to leave Greenville and move to Mexico."

"How many jobs?" I asked.

"Twenty-seven hundred."

"Remind me, what's the population of Greenville?"

"Eight thousand. The town has grown up around the factory."

Jennifer M. Granholm and Dan Mulhern,

A Governor's Story

Electrolux Moves to Mexico

He didn't hide.

An English teacher referring to the
president of the Montcalm Community
College at the time of the plant closing

For a century, Greenville, northeast of Grand Rapids in Montcalm County, near the center of Michigan's lower peninsula, had been home to the world's largest refrigerator plant. Now, the plant was in the hands of a Swedish appliance conglomerate, Electrolux. The other main employers in town were Federal-Mogul and Tower Automotive, as well as suppliers of Electrolux. While Governor Jennifer Granholm attempted to put together a significant incentive package to keep the company in Greenville, in the end the company president told her, "There's nothing you can do." Electrolux closed the facility and moved to Mexico in 2006.

Montcalm Community College Embraces Its New Students

I knew we needed to create a place where people could come together. We needed to keep that focus on making things better, even if there were no jobs at the end of the line. The focus wasn't to look at only education and training; we were looking at the lives of these people. First and foremost, there was economics. How do you plan financially when there will no longer be income? There was trauma and pride. Most of these people did not see themselves as the kind of people who used these support agencies. They didn't want to go to school. They wanted a job. They had eighteen months of benefits. I knew this (education) was not their priority.

Former Montcalm Community College President, Don Burns

President Burns of Montcalm Community College knows a few things about dislocated workers. Thirty years ago he had conducted research for his doctoral dissertation on a group of close to nine hundred people, mostly women, who lost their jobs at a Chrysler plant not far from Greenville. Most of the workers were not young and had tons of seniority. Some had no interest in getting training for new jobs since many had spouses who worked and they did not have to support the family.

When Electrolux closed, Don had a feeling for what would happen. He knew that what happened to the workers would depend, in large part, on what kind of support system they had. He was not speaking of the social service agency kind of support. He was talking about the family support system. Some would want to use the college's resources. How many would come?

Don thought people in the community and at the college needed to know some things, so he brought in a speaker:

> We didn't know what it meant to be driven into poverty. A minister in the community had lost a farm early in his life. He was so eloquent and kind about what we would see: "You will see anger, but it's fear and it's shame."
>
> President Don Burns

College staff really didn't know what to expect. Don describes the situation "like a cow going through a snake." What processes and procedures were they going to have to redesign? How do you redesign an institution during a crisis?

One thing was clear to him. They were not going to be able to handle all of the deficiencies and missing pieces. For instance, one of the biggest challenges the college faced was the overwhelming number of people who did not have their General Education Diploma (GED). This was because in earlier years at the plant, people did not need to possess a high school diploma or GED to be hired. A large number of people dropped out of high school and started working at Electrolux at the first possible opportunity. Some started as young as sixteen.

"We were overwhelmed by the number of people who did not have a GED. This problem was bigger than we were," Don said.

College staff wanted to take ownership of this problem and start a GED training program. "That's admirable, but not realistic," Don said. He had to explain to them that this piece was not their cross to bear.

In Michigan in the mid-1990s, adult basic education was transferred from the public schools to the workforce development system. There is no uniform system in the country for adult basic education. It can be found in K–12, community colleges, or workforce development agencies. As it turned out, the workforce development agency in Greenville had to lease space in a building and add more seats in order to accommodate the overflow crowd when they ran out of room at the job center for those who needed adult basic education.

The biggest challenge for the college turned out to be the skill level of many of the students, adequate curriculum for the job market, and the schedule.

> You simply don't know what you are going to be
> doing. All you know is what you have been doing."
> Faculty and staff dug in and made suggestions by
> asking, "What if we…could do this?" They did not
> say, "No, we can't do that."
>
> President Burns

Admissions: Getting Students in the Door

Debra Alexander began her new job in admissions at Montcalm in September 2004. In December, a trickle of new students would soon become a flood. "I hadn't settled into a routine yet," said Debra. Maybe that was a good thing. The college normally had fall enrollments between 1,500 and 1,600. In fall semester 2004, enrollment hit 2,080. Over three years, that number would swell to 2,717. The fact that the highest enrollments came later would not be that unusual where a company announces its closing a few years out and workers have over a year of benefits. Electrolux was a union shop, and workers had UAW benefits upon losing their jobs.

Debra began one-on-one appointments with the workers. She started at eight in the morning and finished the appointments at four in the afternoon. Day after day, she helped students find appropriate classes. She did her regular work after four, sometimes getting home at nine or ten at night. Every counselor and admissions person was booked solid. In fact, two part-time registration people had to be hired. They had to bring in more help to the financial aid office, as well.

> They [students] needed to talk. With few ex-
> ceptions, they should have had counseling. They
> were used to a certain lifestyle and suddenly it was

gone. Sometimes, both husband and wife came. Half of the appointment was spent discussing their personal issues. They seemed to be in shock and sad. Toward the end, I got more angry students. I don't know how we did what we did. In looking back, I was not ready to hang myself. However, now we are doing group interviews as opposed to one-on-one.

Debra

To make matters more complicated, most of these new students had not had to use a computer at work or at home. At Montcalm, students usually used the computer kiosk to register for their classes online. This was not going to work for these students.

We had to introduce a new class on computer basics. Most did not have experience with a computer. We had to get them over the "I'm going to blow it up if I touch this key" syndrome. I helped them by showing them how to sign up for classes. Some at the college felt we were enabling them. They said, "You can't do this for them." But when you see the fear in their eyes, you didn't care what other people thought. I felt, in the long run, what mattered was that they focused on their studies.

Debra

Further, they were terrified and believed they were too old. They mentioned the word "rusty" a lot. They said they were too intimidated to be in a classroom. Fear was the major emotion.

I still remember the shock on the faces. This is my most significant memory. I feel like to be able to sit down and say to them, "It's going to be OK," made them feel less scared.

Debra

The lines of communication between Michigan Works (the workforce development agency in the state) and the college were open and used frequently. The workers would come to the college with a sheet they had received at Michigan Works that looked like the results of a career aptitude test. The students would come in and hand Debra the sheet, and she had the distinct feeling that they didn't seem to have been counseled or debriefed on what was on the sheet. The Michigan Works staff was overwhelmed, and the students were very confused. Debra felt that they were given too much information in a short period of time. The caseworker-coaches would say that the student misunderstood. If the students weren't sure what their career results were, they were given the Discoverer Test with the counselors and then debriefed on the results. Many students chose to study business because it fit a lot of job options and was general enough to open a lot of doors.

Students had to have a full-time schedule, or twelve credit hours, in order to remain eligible for training dollars. This was essentially four courses per semester. This was too much for these students, but the counselors and admissions people tried doggedly to accommodate this requirement. First, they had to find courses that did not have prerequisite courses. Plus, courses did not have reading level prerequisites, either, and Debra knew that she might be putting students into classes that were too sophisticated for them. Most students tested into developmental or remedial courses. Some even tested below basic skills level, which would be below a fourth-grade level. There was no instruction at this low level of basic skills at the college, so students were put into courses that represented the very lowest level of remedial.

The Classroom: Teaching and Learning

> I think the college was very keenly aware that we were going to be the lifeline with these people. Some of them should not have been taking full loads. My sense is that most of them experienced a tremendous amount of pain and stress. Sometimes, the frustration was directed toward me.
>
> Joel , Instructor

Joel Brouwer had been at Montcalm Community College for ten years at the time of the Electrolux closing. He taught oral and written communications courses. One of his evening classes at the time was predominantly made up of either Electrolux workers who had lost their jobs or students who had a family member or a friend who had lost their job. It was hard not to be affected by this closing. What he distinctly remembers about this group of dislocated workers is their need for clear instructions. "You tell me what to do, and I'll do it," a student said. They were accustomed to people telling them what to do. They had plant supervisors who told them exactly what to do. They had people at Michigan Works who told them what to do. The need for clear instructions was a big deal. Trying to "figure things out on their own" was a bit of a challenge.

This characteristic became apparent in one of the first assignments, which was to write an essay on a stressful experience. "How many words?" a student asked. The question took Joel by surprise. Usually the last question he got was about the number of words. Usually questions were about the subject matter (e.g., Could it be a stressful relationship, a stressful job, a stressful family situation?) How many words? "I don't know," he said. "You are the teacher, you should know!" said a student.

They demanded precision. Joe realized he was contributing to their stress: "In the world they came from, 'figure it out' was disrespectful." Joel became precise.

One of the other areas of stress, again, was when the assignment required the use of the computer. Joel taught one of his courses in a classroom with twenty-four computers. He remembered one occasion at the beginning of the semester when this group of students walked into that room and saw the computers. Some had a look of abject horror on their faces. They turned around and looked for another class. Joel tried to be reassuring to those who stayed, and they survived. Overall, instructors spent a considerable amount of time working with these students and their computer phobia.

> The entire issue with comfort with the college
> classroom…the students said, "I never thought this
> would happen to me. I never thought I would have
> to go back to school again. I hated high school." So,
> not having computer skills was one small part of that
> struggle…not knowing how things worked in college.
>
> Joel

This experience enhanced future instruction, according to Joel. Prior to enrolling these students, fear associated with use of the computer was not as big an issue; now, the college has gotten much better at working with this obstacle and has made appropriate changes. Staff became aware of what they were going to have to teach in the future.

Self-Esteem and Survival

Joel observed another interesting phenomenon with this group, which he referred to as "survival skills":

> They found each other. They would talk about
> their experiences in the shop in class. They would

write about "unreasonable supervisors." Then, on break, you would see them talking informally. The next class session, they would sit next to each other, trios, pairs, etc. They formed connections. The one that was stronger would shepherd the one who was struggling.

Joel said the lack of self-confidence was a real limiting factor. On the whole, in the beginning, the hard-core workers from Electrolux didn't think they could do much of anything beyond making refrigerators. They told Joel that they had "washed out" of writing and math in high school. They truly believed they had no capability to write an essay. Joel told them to write an essay about how they washed out of writing in high school. In the beginning, he admits, he was not nearly sensitive enough to their anxieties. "I did things the way I had always done them," he said. "Now I can see that this was not good."

Joel also took a beating from his students. Sometimes they would say, "You want me to do what?" They didn't see the inherent value in his communications class. They would say, "I have two years of funding. You need to teach me job skills. Why am I doing this?"

> They needed to have enough language to generate a report at work. But they still were skeptical. I had to tell them that these skills lead to growth and thinking capability that will allow them to present themselves better.
>
> Joel

Joel finally describes one student who, although very capable with strong writing skills, still felt that he was wasting time in college:

I encouraged him to enter a writing contest and take the succeeding course. He said, "I just want to get out of here." He was making Bs without much effort. He was in his forties. He said he just wanted to get on with his life. He was what I called the hard-core "I-don't-want-to-go to school" type.

The Age Factor

With such an influx of older students, the average age at Montcalm went up dramatically. One of the classroom dynamics that played itself out, then, was the interaction between the traditional younger students and these older students. Some students in Joel's classes were high school students receiving dual credit, and they were pretty intimidated by the older students. And on the other hand, the older students, once they got comfortable, were not shy about expressing their opinions to the younger learners. This did not always make for great camaraderie in the classroom.

One younger student in a class started to list all of the reasons she could not get her homework done. One of the older students said, "How many hours do you work?" When the student said twelve, but she had a boyfriend, too, the older student had had enough. "This is my schedule: I come to school full time, I have four kids, I study twenty-five hours a week, and, oh, by the way, I'm getting really good grades!"

Changes in Teacher Behavior

Joel worked very hard to keep students from dropping out. "If you are starting to struggle, the worst thing you can do is to disappear," he told his students. "If you talk to me about it, we can work it out." Most did approach him if they were having trouble, but he became particularly aware of signs that a student might not persist. He did a better job of communicating with them. He only lost two or three students in each of his classes.

I tried to put myself in their shoes. I realized they were in a foreign environment, so I tried to imagine what it would be like in their shop. We started to process more explicitly. Everyone has a voice, I said. We respect everyone's voice. Everyone is entitled to an opinion, but opinions have to be backed up by reason. We made other processes in class more visible. I had to be very aware of my procedures and voice them. The students would hang on every word. Their work ethic was incredible, and once they knew what was expected, they would do it. That's how they operated.

Joel

One significant event that was a part of Joel's memory. Many news outlets came to town at the time of the Electrolux closing. One member of the media was David Brancaccio from *Bill Moyers Journal* who taped a segment shot at Huckleberry's Restaurant on Main Street in Greenville. On February 5, 2004, the segment aired. One of the strong feelings that came through in the segment, also echoed in Joel's class, was that folks blamed the North American Free Trade Agreement (NAFTA) for the closing of the plant. Once NAFTA was passed, the Mexican and Canadian borders were opened to trade across.

In Joel's English 101 class, one of the students was a forty-five-year-old supervisor at Electrolux. He knew he was going to lose his job. He and others in the class blamed outsourcing on Electrolux's ability to take the jobs to Mexico. Typically, in this class they write papers on various topics. They discussed the current economic situation, and decided they would research and write about outsourcing.

They did research and, typically, they did a panel discussion at the end of the semester. In groups of two to three, they would discuss and write a joint paper. Some of the groups focused on NAFTA, outsourcing, world economics, etc. It was especially gratifying to see the presentations. They were still angry, but came to realize that world economics is not easy. Whereas before they said, "Everything would be great if we hadn't joined [NAFTA]," now they saw the complexity of it. With these issues, there is no such thing as a right or wrong answer.

Joel

In the final analysis, this was not a bad outcome for Joel's students. For many other students, they found out they could do things they thought they couldn't do. They thought they were no good at "this learning stuff," but they were, and they even liked it. Some said that coming to Montcalm was the best thing that happened to them. And, when defining success, Joel thinks the majority achieved success, because they found out they could do something they thought they couldn't. It did wonders for self-esteem.

The Second Round: A "Green" Plant Brings Hope
In 2006, the Michigan-based company United Ovonics Solar, owned by Energy Conversion Devices, needed to expand its capacity to fill their orders. Their choices of new sites were South Carolina and Greenville, Michigan. Each state compiled an incentive package, and the company, according President Burns, said they chose Greenville because of the ability of Montcalm Community College to develop their workforce. And, develop they did.

Teaching Technical Skills
Chuck Glise had a chemical engineering background and was brought to the college six months after Electrolux closed in January 2006. He was brought in to teach physical sciences, chemistry, engineering technology, integrated manufacturing, and machining.

He was also one of the instructors involved in teaching a new curriculum when United Ovonics Solar (USO) came to town. USO manufactured amorphous film for solar panels that would be used by European countries and municipalities. It began to build two plants in Greenville in 2006, and employment began in 2007.

Chuck had a lot of teaching experience, both in K-12 and post-secondary education. He had worked in many plants and he "was always led in the direction of working with the hourly people." His father did not have a degree but had told Chuck, "The people on the floor can tell you when something is wrong."

When he started teaching a group of thirty students who were receiving skills instruction so that they could work at USO, he felt very comfortable:

> It is much easier to teach here than high school. It is easier because there is a light at the end of the tunnel. They know they are going to get there. I taught a chemistry class, and I knew in October all of these people were going to make it. The class was not over until December. There was a 97 percent pass rate. When you have someone who is motivated, it changes the characteristics of the class.
>
> Chuck

As with Joel's students, these students "found each other," too.

> They helped each other. They did a good job with study groups. My first class was "Math for Electronics." They did all of the problems I asked them to over Labor Day weekend. I got an earful...it was way too much to ask of them. They said they didn't go to the

> Labor Day picnic or camping. They stayed home and
>
> did the problems at the end of the chapter.
>
> Chuck

Chuck became more reflective about the extent of the work he was assigning. These were very good students. They did not struggle with technical reading. They had taken the placement test prior to being assigned to this group. In this respect, USO was able to choose from the cream of the crop. Two-thirds of these students got jobs at the plant.

Joel's oral communications class was important to USO, too. The company was looking for social intelligence. When they interviewed these applicants, they gave them scores for team skills.

The learning went both ways in Chuck's classes. The manufacturing experience of this group of students helped him teach, often referring back to plant operations:

> Things like quality assurance or statistical process
>
> control, I discuss them. These students had some of
>
> these experiences. I drew from the experience they
>
> had. I felt comfortable with this. These students had
>
> a broader base of experiences, and they could help
>
> me explain.
>
> Chuck

But every once in a while, Chuck had to reinforce why they were doing something in particular:

> Why are we counting electrons? I had to reinforce
>
> why this is important and [how it] will lead to some-
>
> thing else which is more important. I don't apologize

for physical science or how things work. For the most part, this was not a problem. This becomes electronics and how to read a meter, I would say.

There were two levels of employment at USO: technicians and production. The technicians had to run the machines and know how to use a computer. The production team did lower level work on the cells. Chuck was preparing the technicians. They had a higher competency level that the company was seeking.

In the end, it was the notorious Midwest work ethic that got students through the program, said Chuck:

"I can work at this and master it," the students said. I didn't have a person who said they couldn't do it. Only one left the program early on.

A Student Perspective

The frustrating part was just that I felt so inadequate. It had been four or five years since I had taken a class. Before, I took one course at a time. Now, I had to take twelve credits, or three courses at a time, at a minimum.

Cindy, Student

Cindy Enbody, a student in her sixties, started working on the production line at the Wolverine Shoe factory in Rockford, Michigan, at the age of eighteen. She got married, had a child, and in 1966 started working at the plant that would become Electrolux. She bid and worked in many different jobs, including inspection, stock, production, parts, and warehouse. She knew the jobs well.

When she was growing up there was no push in her family toward going to college, but she began taking classes because she wanted to further her education. She was interested in geography, history, and the environment and ended up accumulating about twenty credits or so.

> There had been rumors that the plant would close in the 1960s when I started. The plant had changed hands several times. The only thing that made a difference this time was NAFTA. When that law was passed, I knew the writing was on the wall. They gave us two years notice. It was still devastating to a lot of people.

She was close to retirement age when the plant closed. She went to the local job center, and she said she was give three choices of career fields: criminal justice, health care, and education. She started out in criminal justice, but didn't like her instructor and she was told that there was a requisite self-defense class. She didn't think she was up for that. She turned to education courses instead.

Cindy was a perfectionist and was used to getting good grades. This time might be different, and this was extremely stressful for her. Not only did she have to take these courses quickly because she had to be finished in two years, but she had to take eight credits in the summer. The summer experience was even worse because a twelve-week class was condensed into eight weeks.

Furthermore, what was a person who is in their late fifties/early sixties to do about going back into the job market? At each institution, across the board, students who were Cindy's age were skeptical that they could get hired. While many employers stated they would welcome older workers because of their work ethic and maturity, it wasn't clear that the welcome mat was always out for graduates who had gray hair. One day at the job center, for example, it wasn't clear to Cindy that the hiring person from a company's human resources department who was conducting interviews got the message:

I fully intended to work again. I applied and put in my application a few places. I know there was age discrimination. I had an interview in Greenville at the job center. They [other interviewees] had been lining up since early morning. I got to the front of the line late morning. The employer rep had a part they wanted you to put together and three blueprints. I knew how to read the blueprint because I had to learn when I was an inspector. I had come to the college to take a blueprint reading for precision tools class. He [the company rep] told me, "You are the first person today who knew how to read a blueprint." I still got rejected. There were no teaching jobs, either.

It didn't matter to Cindy that there were students of all ages at the college, though:

My daughter thinks I should come to college again. I never thought I was too old. I saw people in their eighties in the news (getting a degree). I thought if they can do it, I can, too. Some of the [younger] students called me "smarty pants." I asked questions and participated. There were a few students who I still haven't figured out how they made it at all. They didn't show up or were late.

The older ones were there to get that degree and some of them worked hard and still wouldn't excel. The younger students had to learn that mom and dad were not looking over their shoulders. I couldn't see wasting the opportunity . I figured we were paying for this as taxpayers.

Cindy saw her fellow displaced workers go myriad directions. Not wanting to go back to school, the majority of Electrolux people did not come to the college. Most just went out and looked for another job, but the pickings were slim. When the Electrolux plant closed, the workers were unionized and making $18.50 an hour. No other jobs out there were paying that hourly wage.

Quite a few [people] went to Meijers. I know some who went to Walmart. They have to do more than just greet these days. They have to do returns, too. I talked to one guy there. He had his journeyman's card from Electrolux and they had him cleaning the bathrooms.

One success story of an older student getting a job was one of Cindy's neighbors who took the medical field track. She had to take many science classes, a math class, and in chemistry she had to memorize the Periodic Table of Elements. She went to Grand Rapids, thirty-five miles away, to work at a hospital as a coder. She was in her early fifties, and she was not eligible for a pension.

Overall, Cindy knew she was fortunate. She had a retirement benefit and her husband had a disability benefit. Her children were grown, so there were not any extra mouths to feed, and she never had to make really tough decisions when it came to finances. She knows of others who are still struggling:

If their unemployment ran out, they didn't have the money to keep their car going, and they needed a car to go to school. A lot of times it meant the difference between gas and food. I don't know what I would have done if that was me.

The Global Economy Strikes Again

In 2012, Joel's communications students got another lesson in global economics. This one could extinguish all hope for their community's economic revival. For a small Midwest community of 8,000 to get slammed once may not be news anymore, but to be victimized twice within a five-year period is galling. This is what happened to Greenville, Michigan.

The two new USO plants sat neatly side by side in a small industrial park on the city's east side for three years. In 2010 and 2011, USO began experiencing difficulties, in part because of the global recession but also because China entered the market for solar panels. European countries and municipalities that were customers of USO cut back on their orders. By November 2011, employees were being furloughed. In February 2012, the company declared bankruptcy. By March 2012, equipment was being auctioned off to the highest bidder.

As bad as this may seem, the good people of Greenville and Montcalm Community College stand ready to gear up for the next global business to come to town. And if that business doesn't come, at least these displaced workers will have received an education and taken charge of their futures.

PART III – Ivy Tech: Industry-Based Credentials

The Place: Indianapolis, Indiana
The Plant: Navistar to PurePower, LLC
The College: Ivy Tech-Indianapolis

> The community came together
>
> Danny, UAW Representative

The Indiana Automotive Industry

Before the Great Recession, the auto industry in Indiana was in the throes of restructuring—applying new, cleaner technologies and production efficiencies, reducing costs, and modifying product lines to equal or beat global competitors—accompanied by an extended period of downsizing since 2006. Overlaying the recession and the restructuring, though, compounded the challenges the industry was already facing: the skills of the workforce.

According to *Driving Workforce Change: Regional Impact and Implications of Auto Industry Transformation to a Green Economy*, auto industry workers needed higher-level skills for new vehicle technologies and the green economy. Post-secondary education and technical training would be required for these workers to transition into new occupations. And because Indiana had a high percentage of engine manufacturing jobs, it would be critical to the state that these workers receive appropriate training.

The problem was that over half of the dislocated workers only had a high school education or less. For those who lost jobs, would they be able to upgrade their skill levels in order to go back into this industry? How long would it take?

Because of the demographics of the Indianapolis automotive industry, a large percentage of workers who were downsized were able to retire. Others had enough years of seniority to bump other automotive workers and take jobs in different plants in other cities, such as Fort Wayne, Indiana. But what about those workers who were left, those not even close to retirement and without the seniority to take other jobs in other cities? This was the plight of hundreds of workers who lost their jobs at Navistar International Corporation's Indianapolis Casting and Engine plants.

Job Center Blues

In 2009 the WorkOne system, part of the Job Services Division of the Indiana Department of Workforce Development (much like Wisconsin), was so overwhelmed by the numbers of unemployed workers coming for services that paper work got severely backlogged. Applications for benefits were taking longer, and for people who were living paycheck to paycheck, this meant zero to very little income.

To help with paper work processing, WorkOne turned to UAW workers at the union hall. One of those people was Danny Ernest, a former skilled plant tradesman and UAW representative covering the states of Indiana and Kentucky:

> In July 2009, people couldn't get other jobs. There were none. Sometimes, it seemed as if the automotive worker benefits were taking longer to process...almost as if this was intentional. I saw grown men cry when their benefits were delayed.
>
> Plus, all applications had to be completed by the worker on the computer. Many of these guys had never used a computer. I helped with this. Some WorkOne employees thought I was coddling these workers. I didn't care. The stress level I saw in the eyes of these workers was enough for me to want to help them.

While Danny was working with these UAW workers and their benefit applications, he was also working on a plan with other community members to bring new life to the old plant.

History of Navistar's Closing

In January 2009, Navistar International Corporation announced it would close its Indianapolis Casting Corporation subsidiary by July 31. This was a result of the termination of a thirty-year supplier arrangement with Ford Motor Company. The plant produced gray and ductile iron engine blocks. Between the foundry and the adjacent diesel engine plant, 1,250 jobs were to be eliminated. These were the UAW workers who Danny served at the job center.

Between July 2009 and July 2010, a good thing happened. The community came together to negotiate a new five-year UAW contract to keep the casting plant open. The new contract cut workers' wages, vacation time, and holidays, but it preserved a number of positions for production workers and skilled tradesmen. The goal at the time of the contract was to attract new business to the plant. Danny was on the front lines of both of these efforts.

As part of the Obama Administration's emphasis on clean automotive emissions, the federal government was looking for a partner to produce cleaner diesel engines. Grants were available to produce new compacted graphite iron diesel engines. The community, including the mayor and congressional representatives from Indianapolis, lobbied to have those engines produced locally. Thus, PurePower Technologies LLC, a Navistar company, came to town. The plant is one of the few remaining facilities in the country that make automotive engine blocks and heads. But this was a more advanced manufacturing plant. It needed workers with advanced manufacturing skills.

The Community College System to the Rescue

Indiana's community college system is called Ivy Tech, and it is Indiana's largest provider of workforce training solutions. For thirty years, the college has provided training services to Indiana employers through its Division of Workforce and Economic Development. It is nationally known for its emphasis on developing the workforce in manufacturing. It does this, in part, through a system of industry-recognized credentials, or certificates, which usually do not have academic credit attached to them.

Ivy Tech-Indianapolis learned of the closing of Navistar in January 2009. They already had programs developed by business and industry for people needing new skills in advanced manufacturing facilities.

> We are in a market change. When PurePower Technologies began re-hiring a certain number of people back, even though the leadership was the same, they were not interested in hiring a lot of people back. They were very focused on hiring people who had good basic academic skills and good reading and writing. This could be the skill set for the future.
>
> Scott Horvath, former dean of Workforce Development, Indianapolis

Ivy Tech and Danny Ernest went to work screening people who could be trained for this higher-level work. Those who didn't qualify went right into computer training. Some classes were sixteen hours, but most were more. The college trained close to four hundred workers on computers alone, the emphasis being to get them at the point where they could send an e-mail.

Higher-Level Instruction

One of the training programs manufacturing employers wanted and Ivy Tech used was Workplace Advantage. Workers were given the adult basic skills tests. Employers were looking for reading levels that were at approximately the ninth- to tenth-grade level as well as communication and computer skills. The Advantage program consisted of computer applications, basic shop math, advanced shop math, business basics, and Purdue-sponsored lean (efficiency in process) manufacturing. One of the biggest complaints Ivy Tech got from employers was that workers did not know how to do simple things like read tape measures or use instruments, so an additional class was added for this. Business basics, in particular, was included for a specific purpose:

> We put in a business basics class so that the workers could look at the shutdown situation from a business perspective. Some workers took these shutdowns very personally. We had a simulation or game they had to play involving a chocolate plant. You have a product and a customer and immediate decisions to make...good or bad. There is nothing personal involved in making any of these decisions.
>
> Administrator

The structure of the computer class was also different for a reason:

> We had them in computer classes fifteen hours a week for two weeks. Then, they were two weeks on their own. Most of them had computers at home. This was a test of sorts to see if they would get the work done on their own at home or would they procrastinate. Down the road, the college and future employer needed to know if these people were disciplined enough to do the instruction on their own.
>
> Administrator

Students also received training for a credential recognized by manufacturing employers called Manufacturing Skills Standards Certificate (MSSC), which consists of instruction in quality, safety, maintenance, and manufacturing processes.

Some of the tracks were aimed at experienced industrial workers who were told they needed to add a new skill to their current skill set. Employers wanted students to be cross-trained, so they could not enroll in a program for a skill they already had mastered. In fact, only workers who had previous industrial work experience could be part of the advanced manufacturing program. These workers were the most successful in gaining higher-level skills. Classes were held sixteen hours a week over eighteen months to get the workers to the skill level needed by employers. Classes were offered face-to-face and online, allowing some workers to work at their own pace. Ivy Tech was particularly fortunate to have a great instructor for math.

> She was an engineering graduate of Kettering University in Detroit. In the math class, she made the students show their work at the front of the classroom on the board. All of the guys did it. They weren't embarrassed, even though this was putting them in an awkward position. She had a great understanding of the subject matter and the ability to teach. She was one of those teachers who could probably teach any subject matter.
>
> Administrator

Success

For the Indiana students, success was more tangible and came in the form of industry-recognized credentials. As of June 2011, approximately sixty-four people qualified for training and received national certifications to allow them to go into a new workplace with new credentials. One hundred percent received at least one of the four MSSC certifications. Fifty-six percent completed all four of the MSSC courses to receive their Production Technician Certification. Eleven students received American Welding Society certifications, and 87 percent of the students enrolled in the advanced manufacturing track earned the National Institute of Metalworking Skills (NIMS) Certification in Safety, Metals and Materials.

The classrooms at the end of the line for these Indiana students prepared them to return to manufacturing environments and, in particular, automotive industry plants. At the end of the day, they had expanded and improved their skill sets so that they were not going to be at the mercy of any one employer again. This was the beauty of going back to the classroom to obtain these advanced manufacturing skills. Ivy Tech had cornered the market on this model of non-credit instruction, and for their employers and students, it worked.

PART IV - Commentary

The Ships: Relationships, Partnerships, and Leadership (You Cannot Sail without Them)

Relationships

Student success in college is based on many factors. One of them is supportive relationships formed while in college, a "bonding" of sorts. This bonding could be between a student and a staff member, a student and a teacher, or a student and another student. These kinds of relationships were particularly important when a classroom was at the end of the line for assembly line workers. Some of these support roles began with a staff person at a job center. If good relationships existed, students were able to accomplish many things. If relationships turned sour, a toxic situation and poor results occurred.

Good relationships were essential and cultivated between college staff and Job Services Center staff. Their job collectively was to make sure students received the assistance they needed to be successful. At every stage of the process, things happened the way they were supposed to or not, often based on the nature of this relationship.

Students and Teachers

Students often used the term "wonderful" to describe their instructors, saying they "wouldn't have made it without them." Students believed teachers were partners promoting their success. Some students still stay in touch through e-mail with their teachers three years after graduation. These are the bonds that were formed.

Behind the scenes, college managers were trusted partners with instructors and staff in resolving problems and issues that arose when students and community were in turmoil. This relationship between supervisor and employee had to be based on honest dialogue because the problems were numerous and often complex.

Students did not necessarily talk about the bond between students, but instructors did. They noticed the nurturing relationships formed among student themselves, particularly for those who were in class together many hours a week. These students became familiar with each other's family, formed study groups, and in all other ways became the cheering section for each other.

All of these relationships combined were responsible for the success of a small group of eleven Medical Laboratory Technician (MLT) students at the Monroe campus of Blackhawk Technical College.

New programs with new instructors are not always a recipe for success, as we have seen. The MLT program was the exception. The campus was fortunate to have a long-tenured, creative and competent administrator who had been leading the campus for more than twenty years. She had taken ownership of her campus and its importance in the life of the Monroe community. She was well-connected, well-respected, and had raised her own children in the community. She sat on the boards of many charitable and cultural organizations in the community. These long-standing, trusting partnerships led to her ability to work with business and industry, health care organizations, and government entities to develop the workforce. She knew what business needed and hired instructors consistent with those needs.

Instructors Steve and Katry were hired to have primary responsibility for the Medical Laboratory Technician program. The administrator knew that having a strong, vital relationship with these new, nervous instructors would be critical to student success. The two turned into extraordinarily gifted instructors, even though neither had previous full-time teaching experience. What these two instructors lacked in teaching experience, they made up for in creativity, motivation, and intuition. Their relationship with their students and with each other would make the difference between success and failure. They knew the students had to learn to trust them, and they worked hard at this task. While it takes time to make a worker into a student, the ultimate test, according to the teachers, was when the students took ownership of their work. One example of this in the

MLT program was an offer by a student to let the instructor share her (the student's) work with the rest of the class because she believed she had done a good job and believed other students could benefit.

At a time in history when the vast majority of community college students do not complete college programs within six years, and approximately 26 percent complete a two-year program in four years or less, the 89 percent success rate of the MLT program would be considered a miracle most unusual. The instructors would say it was the bonding that occurred that made the difference.

External Partnerships

Each of the colleges explored in this book had partners that were critical to their success. Blackhawk Technical College had employer partners who needed its graduates from a number of different program areas. The MLT program cited above is one example of where the external health care facilities that were used as clinical sites could either make or break the program.

One of the most important partners for Blackhawk, however, was the Southwest Wisconsin Workforce Development Board. During the recession, the board received an influx of federal money for training experiences. The college and the Board entered into contracts for instruction totaling approximately $800,000 and worked together to determine which programs served an immediate labor market need. Workers were assessed for career aptitude and placed into groups or "cohorts" in which they would take all of their courses together. The program areas were in industrial fields and health care. Classes were held during times when classrooms were available, usually in the afternoon. Each class had approximately eighteen to twenty students. Like the MLT program at the Monroe campus, these small groups of students had success rates much higher than the regular student population. The college and the Workforce Board worked closely, daily at times, to make sure these cohorts ran smoothly. When there were disagreements and conflict between the partners, they were resolved.

Other government support appeared at this time. If there was a silver lining to the cloud that hung over these students during the economic upheaval, it was that other federal government money came to their rescue, including the previously-mentioned allocation from Congressman Herb Kohl. Federal dollars were used, in part, to pay for instruction, equipment, and supplies for the MLT program. Students also received unemployment dollars to sustain them and their families while they went to college, and the state Department of Workforce Development, with federal Department of Labor dollars, provided training vouchers to pay tuition.

Private Support: Zonta to the Rescue

Students in the MLT program had to serve in internships. Eleven students needed internship sites. The instructor had to search far and wide for sites once the local community sites were filled. Sites a greater distance from the college had to be used. Some of them were in bordering states. Most students struggled financially. There was simply not enough money to pay for all household and program expenses, such as gas to drive to internship sites. When this fact was shared with members of a local affiliate of Zonta, a global organization providing service and advocacy to women and girls, they swung into gear. Zonta of Janesville was able to help. Four students had to go long distances for their internship experiences. This meant some were travelling four hundred miles per week. A couple stayed overnight at motels to complete their mandatory internship hours. Members of Zonta purchased $100 gas cards for each of the women who travelled out of state. They could now drive 1,000 miles and not worry about running out of gas.

Business-Education Partnership Model: Challenges and Opportunities

The decision to work with industry seems like a no-brainer. Local businesses and corporations have a vested interest in seeing students succeed. And

community colleges have a reputation for tailoring
curricula to local needs. But forming and maintaining a solid industry partnership takes time.
> Ellen Ullman, "Tips on Working with Industry,"
> *Community College Times*

Not all partnerships with business and industry work out well. Preparing the workforce for health care employment, as described above, is easier because it is a highly regulated occupational area with many licensing exams to assure competence. Preparation of employees for the general workforce is more challenging. Here, employers communicate the exact nature of their skill needs. Community and technical college educators then develop the talent needed. While this sounds easy and straightforward, it is not. These kinds of partnerships are sometimes mired by misunderstanding. Business partners accuse the college of not producing quality candidates or, in the alternative, they complain that it takes too long to produce a quality graduate. Their emphasis is on developing talent quickly.

Educators claim that business and industry people simply do not have knowledge about the nature of the educational process and the sequential nature of acquiring skills and learning. Take the case of our assembly line workers acquiring the communication and interpersonal skills so needed by all employers today. With students who lacked communication as part of their skill set while working on the line for the past seventeen years, the road to acquiring, or at least improving, these skills is longer.

Acquiring technical skills for manufacturing is a long process as well, even if the student's work experience included skilled trades in a manufacturing environment. This past work may have been limited to a particular skill set (e.g., spot welding). This is an example of why the job of delivering instruction is time-consuming, and the learning achieved is based on time on task. Time on task is often the bone of contention. How much time? A request may come to the college as a request for short-term training. Businesses ask for short-term training, but they want someone who is a team player, a good communicator, a problem solver, and a critical thinker, all in less than six months. Businesses seek these skills in entry-level employees. If these skills don't exist in college graduates, they will not make it past the interview stage.

The best business partnerships are those where business employees sit on an advisory committee that meets several times a year to share needs and trends in employment. Committee members often have formed long-term relationships built on trust and credibility with college faculty and staff. By listening to business partners on the committees, college teachers and managers get a glimpse of the current employment situation, the near-term employment situation, and what new skills will be needed in the future.

Such discussions can result in the college purchasing equipment to train students identical to that used by local employers. Also, as a result of these regular advisory meetings, college staff can, if the need exists, plan to add additional competencies to the program, or a second year or track. In order for a second year or additional training to work for students, theoretically, they should be hired after a one-year program as entry-level employees and employers should pay their tuition to go back to school to gain more and different skill sets. Ultimately advisory meeting discussions can result in employers setting up internships as a viable means for students to work part-time in the field and for businesses to showcase their company to students before they graduate.

Many of these plans take time to implement. Time to credential is important, but it depends on the literacy skill level of students coming in the front door. Reading levels for most occupational programs are at tenth grade, for instance. Technical manuals for many occupational programs contain sophisticated text and may require a higher level of reading skill. Business partners have to understand what colleges are up against in the same manner that colleges need to understand the dire needs of business for higher skilled employees. Expansion plans are often delayed because talent is not available to staff facilities. Colleges, as good partners, truly want to produce the best-prepared graduate in the shortest time possible. Recently, they have developed promising practices to speed up student academic literacy by integrating skills (math and communications) into occupational courses. This can eliminate additional semesters of course work.

Leadership and Creating a Sense of Community

Leaders need to be visible, says Harry Peterson in his book *Leading a Small College or University*. He states an important part of a college president's job is to "create a context in which people can establish trusting relationships to help one another do their jobs and to make their work satisfying and meaningful." In order to do this, he says, people in the college need to see the president as one of them. He or she needs to lead from the center. While a leader cannot build a community, a leader can create conditions so that others in the college can build a community.

> You cannot will a community into existence, but you can help create the conditions for a strong community to develop, helping to move people from the isolation of their department to thinking about issues across departments.
>
> Harry Peterson,
> Leading a Small College or University

Peterson also says that during crises, people experience things they hold in common. In the case of economic upheaval in the community, those things include a desire to help others whose lives have been thrown into turmoil. How does a leader help with this: by being seen as part of the community. Peterson reminds us that "in a crises, people look at a leader's heart and humanity, not just the brilliance of their minds."

In *7 Lessons for Leading in Crisis*, Bill George describes crisis situations and the leadership it takes to steer a business when there are very public meltdowns. He could have been talking about crises at a college. A CEO is a CEO, no matter the organization. And a time of crisis is only distinguished by the nature of the elements. Here I have used six of George's lessons and illustrate how they apply to college crises.

Lesson No. 1: Face Reality

Leaders have to be grounded. They have to be able to admit mistakes. They cannot try to be someone they are not. George uses the term "authentic" to describe a good leader during a time of crisis. Leading is a humbling experience. Leaders need to admit that they don't have all of the answers. At a college, for example, not everyone is going to get into a course in the semester they want. Particularly for colleges in times of exponential enrollment growth, mistakes will be made. Things will fall through the cracks, be it a missed communication or an unforeseen consequence of an action. Apologize and fix the problem.

Lesson No. 2: Don't be Atlas

If you are a new leader without much background at the institution, ask for help. While this advice may seem like common sense, for new leaders in particular, it can be difficult. Persons with new authority may worry about being seen as incompetent and weak if they seem to need help. It takes courage to say what you do not know, but it is an admission that subordinates will respect. It is also a good lesson as a role model. During a crisis, novel and unusual things will happen, particularly with students who have never been to college before. Rely on others in the college community to help solve problems.

Lesson No. 3: Dig Deep for the Root Cause

Some problems are systems-based. They have existed for some time, but they were dealt with on a case-to-case basis. Now is the time to really fix the process or practice that is causing havoc. Whether it is long financial aid waits, lengthy admissions processes, an outdated system for distributing book vouchers, or inflexible course schedules based on teacher preference, issues will surface in a heartbeat during times of large enrollment increases.

Acknowledge that these problems require major change and adjustment but that tackling them now is preferable.

Lesson No. 4: Never Waste a Good Crisis

In every organization, there are people who are ill-suited to their current jobs. Realign people where there is need. Some people are very good doing certain kinds of work, but they may be in the wrong position. During the time of crisis, it behooves a leader to make changes to get the best fit for the attributes of college employees. This can be done during the crisis, and if it works out, it can be made permanent. Most leaders are aware of people in the organization who are ill-suited to their job and can make a valuable contribution to the college in a position that better suits their skills.

Lesson No. 5: You're in the Spotlight

When you are in the spotlight as a leader, be "open, straightforward, and transparent." Integrity and honesty must prevail. For example, acknowledge that not every student who came to college from the plant will remain enrolled. There is significant attrition. In fact, most workers in these case studies who came did not stay. Not every student who graduated got a job. Some of those graduates who got jobs upon graduation left those jobs, not necessarily voluntarily. All of these things happened. Only some of them are within our control. No matter how hard we try, we are going to have limited success. All of the factors that determine who our students are and who we are as a college community go into determining our outcome. We try to have the best outcome we can. These are the humbling parts of leadership.

Lesson No. 6: Focus on Winning Now

Student success is the "win" as is an improved relationship among members of the college community. The win for the college comes when students, previous plant workers, walk across the stage at graduation on their way to a higher-skilled job. While in all likelihood it may not be a higher-paying job, as in the case of previous unionized workers, it will be a job that pays consistent with skill level. This is a better and more secure position for these former students.

The win for the college will be in better relationships within the college community. Through continuously acknowledging the good work of instructors and staff during difficult times, college leadership can change the culture of the institution. Thanking employees publicly for their contribution to the college and the community may be something new. For administrators to say a simple "thank you" goes a long way.

Success

What are your measures of success?
Can you accept as a measure of success
that you just keep showing up...

Simply staying on the path, no matter what,
keeping on with your direction...

If we have returned again and again to our
work,

If we take challenges, rather than
avoided them?

Margaret Wheatley, *Perseverance*

Success: What Is it and Who Gets to Decide?

> It is easy to be an optimist about America if you stand on your head because the country looks so much better and so much more inspiring when viewed from the bottom up.
>
> Tom Friedman and Michael Mandelbaum,
> *That Used to be Us*

"Pinched," "squeezed," and "caught in the middle": These are words used to describe the condition of low-skilled workers in this country by authors Don Peck, Steven Greenhouse, and Richard Longworth, respectively. Longworth in *Caught in the Middle* describes these workers as "globalization's have-nots" and "older casualties" of the last century's economy. This was *before* they became students, though. What about those who ventured out to continue their education? How would they describe themselves in a sort of "before" and "after" picture?

The stories in this book are about success and failure, challenge and new opportunities. They could have been told in any part of the country. Research from across the United States reports mixed results on "success" of this kind of job training/college experience, usually defining success by the percentage of students who graduate and get middle wage jobs related to their field of study. Amy Goldstein conducted such research on graduates at Blackhawk Technical College and reported her findings in an article for *Pro Publica*. These appear to be fair assessments on whether taxpayer dollars are being spent efficiently and wisely, but they are not the only measures of success. What about the opinion of the students themselves? What do these former plant workers say about the impact this experience had on their lives? I was only able to identify one study that asks former plant workers about their lives post-plant closure.

A Dislocated Worker Study was conducted by Southwest Wisconsin Technical College after the 1996 closure of the Platteville Advance Transformer plant in Platteville, Wisconsin. Advance Transformer was the largest employer in Grant County. The employees were mostly semi-skilled with an average of over eleven years of longevity and an average wage of $8.80 per hour, 60 percent of the statewide average. Six hundred and twenty employees were laid off.

Ten years after the beginning of the layoffs, Southwest Wisconsin Technical College partnered with Job Services of the Department of Workforce Development to conduct a study on the impact of training and services on the employees involved in this plant closure. Surveys were mailed to 567 former employees, with a response rate of 53.8 percent. Forty percent of those surveyed were former students who had one year or more of further education at Southwest Technical College.

Two topics in the survey were relevant to student success: the impact of education in real economic terms and on quality of life. Workers were asked to compare their current job to their job of ten years prior by stating whether their current circumstance was better, the same, or not as good as their Advance Transformer job. Areas of comparison were in wages, benefits, working conditions, hours, commute, advancement opportunity, and job satisfaction. In all seven areas, the "better" category was scored the highest by the participants who spent one year or more at Southwest Tech versus those who had no further education after closure or only short-term training.

Workers were also asked to compare their current quality of life with life ten years ago at Advance Transformer. The results here also show the impact of education on people. Workers were asked to compare their quality of life in the areas of family time, leisure time, mental health, physical health, standard of living/ economic well-being, stress level, and happiness. In all seven areas, the "better" category was scored the highest by those who had one year or more of further education at Southwest Tech.

Another key finding was that workers with one year or more of education, versus no training or short-term training, earned higher wages. Twenty-five percent earned more than sixteen dollars per hour and 68 percent earned between ten and sixteen dollars per hour. Additionally, 28 percent of these former students had been promoted in that ten-year time span.

One of the main differences about the people in this study compared to students described in this book is that the Advance Transformer workers were not making high hourly wages when they lost their jobs. Ninety-three percent were making more money at the end of ten years. Students from the three colleges reviewed here were earning significantly higher wages at unionized shops at the time of plant closure. The ability of these students to earn a similar hourly amount in their post-college jobs was not guaranteed, nor very likely. If wages earned is not the only measure of success, what is?

All Blackhawk students were asked about their "success" prior to completing their education. Specifically, they were asked if they were different as a result of their education experience, and if so, how? Here's what they had to say:

> **Linda:** I am more of a people person. I've always been a caring person. My whole self-esteem has grown. I have more confidence. I'm not afraid to ask questions; I don't feel that I am "just a factory worker."

> **Rob:** I told them over at the Job Services that I would be a professional student. I like learning.

> **Human Resources Student:** I was a shy woman at first. I see where I was and where I am today. I told the instructor "I'm not leaving."

> **Jeff:** I look at things differently. I have a broader perspective. If I was to quit, it would send a really bad message to my children.

> **Brian:** I forced myself to be more open to new things. I took a leadership role in the honor society

here. I was shy, but I then had to speak in front of people.

Dale: I think we are all teachers. In written communications, I did well. I can put five times more things on paper than in the beginning. Everyday I run into someone I used to work with. I always encourage them.

Zac: Coming here gave me more courage. I think just getting into the learning patterns was different. I now analyze situations. I now look at things in a more educated view. Whereas before I might have looked at things and reacted in a certain way, now I look at the big picture. I have always thought outside of the box, but the courses have helped me.

And, so it goes. Students look at themselves differently and respond to situations differently. They are more social and personable. They communicate better and they analyze situations in greater depth. It would be hard *not* to see these types of changes as all for the better and true indicators of success, not just for the students personally, but for society as well.

The quote at the beginning of this Commentary from *That Used to be Us* alludes to the fact that no matter how much doom, gloom, and despair there may be about America's economic future, there are still people who "did not get the message." They are the people at the bottom of the economic heap who refuse to be left behind and keep plugging away, keep showing up, and quoting from Friedman and Mandelbaum, "with the most complimentary meaning are just too dumb to quit."

Many of the students interviewed for this book are folks who did not get the message. They got another message: While America has fallen behind when other countries are fast approaching us in innovation and economy, they personally do not have to be "global casualties." And while their incomes have fallen, they believe they have risen with newfound self-respect, confidence, and skills.

Some across the country may question the wisdom of continuing to pour money into skills training in post-secondary institutions to the tune of $18 billion annually. Do not tell workers who came out of the plants and into the classroom in south central Wisconsin, Indianapolis, Indiana, or central Michigan that the federal dollars are not being used wisely. They won't agree.

Acknowledgements

I am grateful to the talented authors who took time out of their very busy schedules to give this aspiring author their best advice on the many aspects of writing this book. They are Ann Bausum, Richard Hinckley, Richard Longworth, Kathleen A. Paris, Jasmine Paul, Harry Peterson, and Morris Taylor.

A heartfelt thank you goes to those who shared their stories and others who shared much needed information and advice. They are Rob Phelps, Julie Fink, Larry DePersia, Scott Horvath, Alishe Raider, Danny Ernest, Don Burns, Joel Brouwer, Chuck Glise, Debra Alexander, Cindy Enbody, Mark Peterson, Annette Parker, Steve Bienefeld, Zac Fowler, Dave Gile, Dan Harrigan, Kathi Winker, Dusty Williams, Michelle Lomax, Ruth Wheaton-Cox, Melissa Hilker, Helen Franklin, Lisa Severns, Brian Golhke, Bill Lobenstein, Dale Townsend, Linda Hawthorn, Linda Brown, Chris Pody, Ed Robinson, Darian Snow, Tom Westrick, Steve Conley, Bruce Penny, Erica Speveda, Beth Chambers' Human Resources class, Dale Townsend, Tanya Messina, Julie Patrick, Saddie Gunnick, Phyllis Bickford, Lynn Hanley and Jeff Nyborg.

Finally, I would like to thank my friends and family, whose patience, unwavering enthusiasm, and support for this book kept me going through the rough patches.

Bibliography

Adler, Ben and Judith. *Janesville.* Charleston: Arcadia Press, 2011.

Buffett, Peter. *Life Is What You Make It: Find Your Own Path to Fulfillment.* New York: Three Rivers Press, 2010.

Crawford, Matthew B. *Shop Class as Soulcraft: An Inquiry into the Value of Work.* New York: Penguin Press, 2009,

Friedman, Tom and Mandelbaum, Michael. *That Used to Be Us: How America Fell Behind in the World It Invented and How We Came Back.* New York: Farrar, Straus, and Giroux, 2011.

George, Bill. *7 Lessons for Leading in Crisis.* San Francisco: Jossey-Bass, 2009.

Goldstein, Amy. "Rare Agreement: Obama, Romney, Ryan all Endorse Retraining for the New Jobless—But Are They Right?" *ProPublica,* 2012. http://www.propublica.org/article/rare-agreement-obama-romney-ryan-endorse-retraining-for-jobless-but-are-they right?

Granholm, Jennifer and Mulhern, Dan. *A Governor's Story: The Fight for Jobs and America's Economic Future.* New York: Public Affairs, 2011.

Greenhouse, Steven. *The Big Squeeze: Tough Times for the American Workers.* New York: Knopf Doubleday, 2008.

Hamper, Ben. *Rivethead: Tales from the Assembly Line.* New York: WarnerBooks, 1992.

Indianapolis Star. "Autoworkers Take a Hit to Resume Work." July 15, 2010.

Janesville Gazette. "Did Obama Break His Promise on GM Plant?" August 31, 2013.

Longworth, Richard. *Caught in the Middle: America's Heartland in the Age of Globalism.* New York: Bloomsbury, 2008.

Office, Government Accountability. *Workforce Investment Act: Innovative Collaborations Between Workforce Boards and Employers Helped Meet Local Needs.* Government Report, 2012.

Peck, Don. *Pinched: How the Great Recession Has Narrowed Our Future and What We Can Do About It.* New York: Crown Publishers, 2011.

Peterson, Harry. *Leading a Small College or University.* Madison: Atwood Publishing, 2008.

Southwest Wisconsin Technical College. *Platteville Advance Transformer Dislocated Worker Study.* Platteville: Southwest Wisconsin Technical College, 2007.

Terkel, Studs. *Working: People Talk About What They Do All Day and How They Feel About What They Do.* New York: The New York Press, 1972.

The Daily News. "United Solar Ovonic Headed for Auction." March 29, 2012.

Ullman, Ellen. "Tips on Working with Industry." *Community College Times,* July 3, 2013.

United States Department of Labor. *Training and Employment Guidance Letter No. 15-10.* Government Report, 2010.

United States Department of Labor. *Driving Workforce Change: Regional Impact and Implications of Auto Industry.* Administration, US Employment and Training, 2011.

VandeZande, Jeff. "Close Encounters." *Chronicles of Higher Education,* January 13, 2012.

Wheatley, Margaret J. *Perseverance.* Berkana Publication, 2010.

Zull, James E. *The Art of Changing the Brain: Enriching the Practice of Teaching by Exploring the Biology of Learning.* Sterling, VA: Stylus Publishing, 2002.

Made in the USA
Charleston, SC
07 November 2013